SELF-EXAMINATION

THE PATH TO BEING FREE & STAYING FREE

Ikechi G.M. Akurunwa

Unless otherwise indicated, all Scripture quotations are taken from the *New King James Version* of the Bible.

Book Express Publishing House books may be ordered through booksellers or **www.goexpresspublishing.com.**

ISBN: 978-0-9729525-3-8
Library of Congress Control Number: 2021935811
First printing
Printed in the United States of America
Print information available on the last page.

BOOK EXPRESS PUBLISHING HOUSE

Atlanta, Georgia

DEDICATION:

To the soul that longs to walk daily in victory.

CONTENTS

forward..*v*

Chapter One: Self-Examination *11*

Chapter Two: Laws Of Self-Examination... *29*

Chapter Three: The First Law Of Self-Examination........................ *53*

Chapter Four: The Second Law Of Self-Examination..................... *63*

Chapter Five: The Third Law Of Self-Examination........................ *69*

Chapter Six: The Fourth Law Of Self-Examination......................... *83*

Chapter Seven: The Fifth Law Of Self-Examination...................... *101*

Chapter Eight: The Sixth Law Of Self-Examination...................... *117*

Chapter Nine: The Seventh Law Of Self-Examination................. *125*

Chapter Ten: The Eight Law Of Self-Examination *137*

FORWARD

Next time you are asked, "How are you?" or "How are you doing?" take time to tell the person how you are really doing or feeling. If you are happy, tell the person what you are happy about, and grateful for. If you are struggling with something, or having difficulty in any area of life, tell that person what you are going through. I bet he or she will be surprised by your sincerity and transparency. You yourself may even feel uncomfortable or awkward. Why? Reason is we live unexamined lives. When we ask people, "How are you?" we don't expect authentic answers. When people ask us, how we are doing, we give glib answers that have no bearing to what we are actually experiencing. This is because being authentic calls for radical self-examination.

One of my professors from my doctoral program models radical self-examination and authentic living very well. If you don't want to know how he is doing, don't ask him. If you ask him, "How are you, sir?" He will pause briefly, and then tell you how he is doing. You can tell he lives a contemplative and examined life. However, I will not recommend sharing very personal details of one's life with everyone, and my professor and role model doesn't do that either. Nonetheless, being intentional in answering this frequently asked question will make us take constant stock of where we stand with God and with people.

A hallmark of the present society is being in constant motion. We are jet-setters. A person's life is measured by activity and busyness. Someone has said we have become *human doings* instead of *human beings*. In this yet another inspiring book by

Dr. George MacLean Akurunwa, he challenges us to consider the costs and rewards of self-examination. We are accustomed to focusing on the outward, on performing and producing, but not on who and how we really are. We focus on appearance instead of substance. Yet, the scripture tells us God looks in the heart. We want people to think things are going well with us, even when that is not the case. The extent to which we take seriously the task of self-examination indicates the degree to which we value things that are eternal. If a person's desire is to impress people rather than please God, that person will not submit his or her life to God's correction, standard or scale.

In this book titled, *Self-Examination,* Dr. Akurunwa shows why we fail to examine ourselves. Many times we are presumptuous, self-confident, disobedient, or in denial. Failing to come to grips with the reality of one's situation does not change the fact that we are misaligned with God. The things we ignore or sweep under the rug will eventually manifest themselves. Unfortunately, character flaws, relationship cracks and shoddy jobs produce serious consequences that affect the individual and others as well.

The price of failing to examine oneself is severe. This book shows how marriages, businesses, ministries and careers have been shipwrecked because people failed to pay attention to subtle signs of danger. If we submit ourselves to the searchlight of God's word, the wise counsel of family and friends, the rebuke of loving authority figures in our lives, we can save the ships of lives from capsizing. Since so much is at stake, it behooves us to heed this timely message and wake-up call.
While self-examination is very beneficial, it is also painful. As Scripture tells us, "[t]he Lord disciplines the one He loves, and

He chastens everyone he accepts as his son," (Heb. 12:6). Discipline and chastening are not usually pleasant. Often, we do not want to be chastened or corrected. We avoid admitting our shortcomings, character flaws, besetting sins and poor habits. We'd rather cover them up or excuse them. How often do we justify and excuse rebellious spirit, pride, critical spirit, self-centeredness, laziness, strife and domineering tendency as just our "personality"? God's plan is to conform us to the image of His dear Son. Through self-examination, we are able to cooperate with the Holy Spirit who will mold us into Jesus' likeness.

Many believers want to be used of God to glorify His name. And God desires to use us. Jesus says, "… I chose you and appointed you so that you might go and bear fruit …" (Jn. 15:16). If we are not bearing fruit, it is because the little foxes are destroying the vine. We will not live up to our full potentials in God's hands until we are willing to examine ourselves and allow God to prune us.

In this scripturally-based, well-presented and properly-structured book, Dr. Akurunwa shows us the steps to self-examination. An important strength of the book is that it tells us the 'What,' 'Why' and 'How' of self-examination. It is both an exhortation and a manual. The author shows us that self-examination is not a mystical process that can only be attained by a few. Instead, we can learn to examine ourselves by following the guidelines, steps and principles he lays out. The book is practical and the principles are applicable.

Another invaluable quality that commends this book to the reader is the use of personal narratives and examples. It is a rich offer of biblical truth, personal experiences, practical insights and realistic steps. Young and mature Christians alike, will benefit from the discipline of self-examination. As the Apostle Paul enjoins us, "… let anyone who thinks that he stands take heed lest he fall," (I Cor. 10:12). One cannot agree more with the author that self-examination is "*The path to being free and staying free.*" The message is spirit-inspired and timely. We are shown how to cultivate the discipline of self-examination, even in our busy lives. Knowing the value of self-examination and the danger of living presumptuously, we cannot but stop, take heed and take stock of our walk with God, our relationship with others, and the impact we are making on others.

This is a book for all people, from all walks of life, who want to prevail over the forces that would hold them down in their private and public lives. It is a must-read for all who want to live in freedom, walk in victory, and finish well.

Prof. Bala A. Musa, Ph.D.
Azusa Pacific University

SELF-EXAMINATION

THE PATH TO BEING FREE & STAYING FREE

CHAPTER ONE

SELF-EXAMINATION

But let a man examine himself...
– 1 Corinthians 11:28

One of the most important assignments God gave humanity is the responsibility of self-examination. But man is so preoccupied with what seems important to him that he pays little or no attention to self-examination. He is so distracted by so many things, including the leisure and pleasures of life, that he hardly remembers the God-given charge in 1 Corinthians 11:28 to ***examine himself.***

WHAT IS SELF-EXAMINATION ALL ABOUT?

Self-examination is simply an honest evaluation of your life. It's one of those times in your life that you sit down to systematically examine every part of your life to give yourself the opportunity to improve, correct and re-structure your life. In effect, self-examination requires deliberately engaging the mind, the soul, and the spirit in reassessing and recalibrating your life for the purpose of your physical, social, emotional, material, and spiritual improvement and wellbeing.

Why bother with it?

When things are rosy, most people don't want to be bothered with laws and boundaries that will interrupt their lifestyle. They see self-examination as putting brakes in their lives, demanding attention and reformation to those little foxes that they have been disregarding or ignoring for a long time. They see self-examination as too much of an intrusion or inconvenience because they don't want to let go of things they enjoy doing, even when they know some of them are things that may likely cause problems for them.

Those that ask why bother to fix that minor leak on the roof; why bother to make sure a little cut on the skin does not become a big festering wound, or why bother with the little fires, or with that little habit, they always end up regretting not attending to the problems when they were easy to deal with. Self-examination does an excellent job of putting out little fires and arresting a problem before it blows out of proportion.

Why take regular stock?

Have you ever wondered why some people work so hard but make little or no progress in life? Or, why a good part of our society waits until they have been beaten and battered by bad habits before they retreat into the closet of self-examination or consider going into a rehabilitation center? Have you asked yourself why some gifted people wait until the most precious time of their lives is stolen by avoidable circumstances before they come to their senses? If the truth is told, in certain situations, many do not recover.

Taking stock of your past and what lies ahead of you is one of the ways to escape living a wasted life. *It's important to remember that what you fail to examine today may undermine your future.* Stock-taking helps you to discover problems in your life that need to be addressed before they grow into monsters you cannot defeat. Stock-taking enables you to rethink those actions that negatively impact your life before they become mountains too high for you to climb.

In effect, the absence of stock-taking or a lifestyle of self-examination is one of the major reasons people do not live to their full potential. As simple and basic as self-examination may seem to the casual observer, it carries a lot of transformational power. It is the little rudder that turns a ship in the right direction and saves it from disaster. It wakes up someone from slumber before his life is plundered by ineptitude or by the pilfering hands of laxity. Self-examination is the tiny grain of salt that makes the food of life tasty and sweet. It's the little flame that turns a dark abysmal room into a plethora of heavenly lights. It's a powerful tool in the hands of the wise to loosen the tight knots of any chain of captivity. It's a life-changer; it helps you count the cost of negligence and the unnecessary burden it bestows on those who plough through life daily without self-examination.

The Bible says, **"For which of you, intending to build a**

tower, does not sit down first and count the cost, whether he has enough to finish it— lest, after he has laid the foundation, and is not able to finish, all who see *it* begin to mock him, saying, 'This man began to build and was not able to finish'? Or what king, going to make war against another king, does not sit down first and consider whether he is able with ten thousand to meet him who comes against him with twenty thousand?" (Luke 14:28-31).

Life is like building a tower. It's a journey we start at birth, and without regularly sitting down and counting the cost of living through each day, we will run into a lot of problems as we transition into adulthood. Self-examination allows you to sit down and count the cost of building your life on the treacherous and shifting sand of the earth. When you fail in this formative stage, you may hinder God from building you into a holy vessel that He can use to deliver the dying world around you.

As an emphasis, every Christian is a builder and a building under construction. We are called to build ourselves so that we will be able to develop others and build the kingdom of God. We live amid a crooked and hostile world where different floods of trials and tribulations of life ravage each day. And not to count the cost of building your life, the greatest project God gave you on earth amounts to negligence and recklessness. And what is more, when you don't count the daily cost of erecting the building blocks of your life, you may reduce yourself to an abandoned or neglected property, aborting the great plans God has for your life.

HINDRANCES TO SELF-EXAMINATION

There are so many things that can hinder you from living a daily life of self-examination. Some are very subtle, and some are not. Let us take a closer look at them.

- **Assumptions**

Assuming that you know an area too well and that no navigational tool is needed is the mistake some men make when they want to revisit an area they had visited once or twice before. Men are wont to tell their wives, "I got this!" They assume they can figure out where they are going but when they end up in the wrong place or address, they realize their assumption was wrong. Some hikers have gotten lost because they assumed they knew the trail so well that they could plow through it with their eyes closed, only to find out later they were wrong.

Spiritually speaking also, some Christians feel they know it all. They assume they are too strong to worry about contamination from the world. They arrogate to themselves the power they don't have by assuming they can stop the mouth of every lion or even take up fire with their bare hands and won't get burned. Some of them would do certain spiritually dumb things to prove they have faith, only to end up hurting themselves. Others allow or accommodate friendship with people who have the capability of negatively influencing them or possibly pulling them down (like Judah's king, Jehoshaphat befriending

Israel's king, Ahab – nothing good came out of it!).

Why will you allow an unmarried lady to visit you at the wrong time of the night and assume all will go well? Ask Samson what happened to him when he allowed Delilah to hang out with him for a prolonged period (Judges 16). When pastors are counseling women, it is advisable to have their wives nearby or keep their office doors wide open if their spouses are in other engagements. Pastors, don't assume you are infallible; put on your guards, or you will learn the hard way!

Assumptions are very dangerous. They can lead to very costly mistakes. Do your research very well before you venture into something; otherwise, you may end up biting more than you can chew. Don't assume things. Make sure God is leading you before you dive into ministries, businesses or explore a new territory.

Use the numerous research tools available today to help you discover the hidden dangers you may not know that exist along the way you plan to travel or in the project you want to undertake. Save yourself the pain that stems from negligence and ignorance. Take time each day to stop at the laboratory of self-examination for a closer look at seemingly insignificant things you assume you have under control. With the high magnifying glass of self-examination, you might discover vulnerable areas in your life. Look before you jump or cross the roads of life. Don't assume the roads are always clear and safe.

- **Distractions**

Distraction is something we experience every day. Many times, we don't notice how often we are distracted because it's usually very subtle and seemingly insignificant. It's not a coincidence that at the very time you are mulling over an important decision in your life, a visitor or a phone call comes interrupting, and you end up putting off or suspending the rest of the plan. The truth is that you may never revisit it again. If you are driving on the highway and you keep getting distracted, you may end up crashing and not getting to your destination. That's what happens in our lives. Most of the disruptions in our lives or the mistakes we make could be traced to distractions, the secret destructive assaults we hardly notice.

Distraction is one of the greatest tools of the devil. He knows when to strike. Pay attention to those distractions that come each time you start doing things that will add value to your life; those distractions are not ordinary. Distractions that rob you of the time you need to evaluate a project before jumping into it or steal the time you need to review an offer made to you before accepting it are not ordinary.

If you are spiritually alert, you could discern which interruptions are sent to cause disruptions in your life or to save your life. The devil plays this game of disruption and diversion very well with women when it comes to marriage. Many times, when God has given a sister a wonderful brother to marry before they go to the altar, the devil comes with his candidate. Remember, the devil's motive is always to steal, kill or destroy

(John 10:10). When the devil presents his candidate, he intends to distract the sister and lure her away from the right brother. Usually, he brings a richer and more handsome man than the brother she knows God is leading her to marry. Unfortunately, many sisters have failed the test and made a shipwreck of their Christian faith and lives.

Satanic distractions are not peculiar to sisters only. The devil throws red herrings also to brothers. There was a case that broke my heart recently. A devout pastor visited our local church in Atlanta, and immediately he set his eyes on a sister who had divorced twice; he fell for her. He quickly dumped the sister he had already promised marriage. Shortly after, he got married to his newfound love. A few months later, they moved from Atlanta to another city. There they successfully built a dynamic and vibrant church. Within a few years, they were able to establish two other branches. On the surface, things looked great, but a severe fire was brewing underneath. One day it erupted and boiled over to the point that nothing could put it off. Before they divorced, I visited the pastor and the wife. You could hardly tell there was anything wrong with their marriage. The sad part of the story is that the man asked for a divorce after he could no longer endure his wife's tormenting spirit.

After the divorce, they took the fight to the streets. The woman that was once his wife spilled the whole beans and washed their dirty laundry in the open for all to see. It was very disgusting. It resulted in the closure of all the church branches, and since then, the pastor has not found his footing again.

Every day, we are on a driving course down the tortuous road of life. Don't let distractions cause you to take your eyes off the road. Don't be a victim of an avoidable accident. Self-examination helps keep your eyes on the road; it helps you stay focused all day and all night as you navigate the rough terrains of life.

You carry a lot of treasures in your hands; don't let any distraction cause them to slip off your hands. If you value your life, then try and keep it on course. Refuse to be lured away from Victory Lane by irrelevances such as the pursuit of fame, money, power, and other perishable commodities that cannot buy you a ticket to heaven.

- **Work Load**

When you are too busy, you have no time for anything. Sometimes we get so drowned by our workload or family problems, or ministry challenges that we have no time for self-examination or introspection. And by the time we realize what our self-imposed workload is doing to us, we have been injured. How many times have you asked yourself, "How did that happen? I cannot believe I did that! How can I, a pastor or a great community leader do such a thing?"

Don't ever think the world or your company will not continue if you don't put in twenty hours of your time each day. Don't ever think you can solve the problems of the whole world or that you are indispensable. Don't destroy your life trying to solve a problem meant for twenty people, or spend all your time trying to impress your friends and enemies. Create the time for you to rest and to examine your life. It will help you to build a more substantial hedge of protection around yourself. Don't think only you have the panacea for the world's problems and end up not having answers for your own problems. The world was here before you arrived, and it will be here by the time you make your exit.

Some people worked so hard to make money but sadly were not alive to spend it. They worked themselves to death by neglecting to take time to rest and to smell the roses. In the end, all their toils were in vain: they were not alive to enjoy the fruits of their labors. A wise man or woman makes time for self-evaluation and for things more important than fame, authority, and money. They take time each day to enjoy their family and prepare for eternity; that journey we would all embark on one day.

- **Excuses**

You may have asked your child why he didn't finish his homework and gotten a catalog of reasons. "Oh, mom, it was because you asked me to wash the dishes; oh mom, it was because dad wanted me to clean my room." That's what we do with God. We have five excuses for something we failed to do or for something we have done wrong. That was what Adam did in the Garden of Eden.

In Genesis 3:11, God asked Adam, **"Who told you that you *were* naked? Have you eaten from the tree of which I commanded you that you should not eat?"** And he answered, **"The woman whom You gave *to be* with me, she**

gave me of the tree, and I ate" (Genesis 3:12). Instead of owning up to his mistake, he shifted the blame to Eve. Unfortunately for him, the excuse wasn't good enough to save him or the woman.

As a pastor or a Christian leader, how many times have you mounted the pulpit on Sunday morning or on Wednesday, unprepared? If God were to ask you, "Why are you here to feed my children junk or leftover food?" What will you answer? Maybe, "God, I was busy counseling that sister or that brother." That sounds like a good excuse, but it may not be good enough. Too many of us easily use excuses for our Ponzi schemes because we have failed to take time from our busy schedules to analyze our lives regularly. If we do, we might discover that it is the crack in our prayer life or our selfish ambitions that are causing our problems.

- **Ignorance**

Ignorance can be costly. Ignorance of dangerous objects or harmful environments does not exempt you from their harmful effects if you wander into them. Some people have been electrocuted because they unknowingly fiddled with a dangerous electrical current. Also, many people have hurt themselves while using equipment they were not conversant with. But if they had taken the time to study the manual or to ask questions, they would have avoided the harm they caused themselves.

To explore a dark cave, you need a flashlight. If you didn't know you needed a flashlight in a cave exploration and failed to bring one along, it would not make the cave suddenly light up for you. Life is like a dark cave. There is a lot we cannot see as we wander through its many chambers. So, to explore the cave of life ignorantly, without the Author of light, is to leave your life to chance.

Hosea 4:6 says,
"My people are destroyed for lack of knowledge.
Because you have rejected knowledge,
I also will reject you from being priest for Me;
Because you have forgotten the law of your God,
I also will forget your children."

Spiritual ignorance is very deadly. There are many poisons out there, and if you are spiritually ignorant, you can consume them and get hurt. This is why it is crucial to examine whatever you consume.

Self-examination includes examining things around you and how they can affect you. It includes examining who you allow to come close to you, who you embark on a project with or partner with in a business, or whose material or messages you consume. Many are peddling sugar-coated poisons.

Looks are deceptive. Life calls for carefulness and closer examination before you leap or jump into things. Life calls for caution in a world where darkness has blurred the line between good and evil.

Ignorance does not exempt you from imminent danger when you play deaf to warnings; it does not spare those who refuse to heed important safety instructions or wade through a snake and alligator-infested swamp with disregard to caution or safety. Ignorance is no respecter of persons.

- **Forgetfulness**

How many times have you left home for work, and halfway down the road, you realized you forgot something you will need at work? Maybe, if you had woken up a few minutes earlier, you would have had enough time to pick everything you needed for work before leaving home. Also, if you give yourself enough time to plan or pack for a journey, you will likely not forget something you would need along the way.

If you are a student, you may have forgotten to bring your completed homework with you to class. You remembered it the moment the teacher asked for it. What about forgetting to comb your hair before leaving the house because you were rushing to get to church or the office early? I have done that before. You walk around the office or church, not knowing that people are staring at you and wondering whether you are in your right mind. Sometimes, when you don't take the time to comb your spiritual hair; it will show! The unfortunate thing is that you may be the only one who does not know about your situation.

- **Giving up**

Life can be cruel, very cruel. It can push people to a breaking point, even to the point where some may give up hope and stop fighting or trying to overcome their adversities. They simply resign themselves to fate. You might be thinking there are no such people around you. You may be wrong. The problem is that you are buried in your job or business and could hardly notice the world around you. Or you are too involved with your own problem that you have not paid attention to the hurting world around you.

Ministry is not only preaching or praying for people. Sometimes what is required might be stretching your hands to someone on the bed of affliction and lifting him up to his feet. It could be mentoring a teenager who is confused about life and has no father to turn to. Ministry has been greatly misunderstood. There is more work outside the church than there is inside the church. Unfortunately, we spend too much time inside our churches entertaining ourselves while the world outside is dying in hopelessness.

- **Denials**

If you are a pastor, you would have found out that the most complicated people to render help to are those who deny having the very problem you want them to address. Also, if you have counseled married couples, you would have discovered that no one accepts to be at fault most times. They both live in denial, seeing the other as the problem. When you fail to see your problems, you stand the risk of living and dying with them.

It is important to listen when people politely point out something you are doing wrong. Certainly, some natural-born critics go around pointing accusing fingers at people; or people who harshly criticize others for the fun of it. Watch out for such people and stay away from them. However, have a listening ear. Re-examine what more than two or three persons have complained about you. Take time to do a thorough self-examination; you might discover they were right. Don't ever live in denial. It's like walking down an unsafe pathway with your eyes closed. It's a dangerous thing to do.

- **Pride**

Many things can hinder a man from self-examination; chief amongst them is Pride. And in this poem below, I highlighted some of the silent ways pride can manifest or take hold of us.

Under a whispered word,
under the glance of an eye,
under the remotest thoughts,
you come rearing your ugly head.

Under a sweet smile,
under a subdued laughter,
under a sonorous voice,
you come rearing your ugly head.

Under a simple handshake,
under a reassuring pat,
under a warm embrace,
you come rearing your ugly head.

Over dinners and wines,
over jobs and careers,
over garments and hats,
you come rearing your ugly head.

Over kind gestures,
over hearty compliments,
over cheers and praises,
you come rearing your ugly head.

In endearing stories,
in plain conversations,
in rousing testimonies,
you come rearing your ugly head.

Pride: morning, noon, and evening,
you come rearing your ugly head,
surging like a turbulent sea
from a heart, you have long possessed.

MAXIMIZING YOUR LIFE

Don't let avoidable circumstances of life hinder you from maximizing your potentials. Certain things cannot be ignored if you want to live in the realm of the extraordinary or in the realm of what God has in store for you. Self-examination is one of them. No wise person leaves his door wide open when a tornado is coming; rather, he will lock his doors and windows and even further restrain them with house furniture or any restraining equipment available if he has the time to do so.

Self-examination helps you to close the door of your life to the prevailing evils of our day, and in the end, avert adversity. It helps you to plant your feet firmer on the ground so that you can withstand the hostile winds of trials and tribulations. It creates a safety net you can use to maximize your potentials or launch yourself to a height ordinarily you would not have attained.

A good soldier must be battle-ready at any given time. He cannot afford to be caught without his armors. If you must be prepared or always ready to overcome the wiles of Satan, you must engage in a daily habit of self-examination, making sure there are no stones left unturned; making sure you are not missing any necessary armor. We are involved in a daily warfare, and only the battle-ready soldier can enjoy the daily life of victory.

CHAPTER TWO

LAWS OF SELF-EXAMINATION

I thought about my ways,
And turned my feet to Your testimonies.
– Psalm 119:59

The world is governed by laws. There are natural laws that govern natural events. There are scientific laws, some of which govern the numerous statistical assumptions and claims in various science fields. Among other laws are those enacted by the government, institutions, social clubs, and other associations or bodies. God's spiritual laws are given to guide the steps of man and keep him on a righteous course until he finishes his earthly journey or assignment. Without these laws, the world will be chaotic and probably spin out of control.

Interestingly, there is a group of laws hardly talked about. These are unique laws that I call ***Laws of Self-examination***. They are laws we create by ourselves to govern no one else but ourselves. All other laws are for the general populace, but laws of self-examinations are set up by you and for you only. This is why these laws are very important and demand a closer look.

THE PURPOSE OF THE LAWS OF SELF-EXAMINATION

1. Governance

Laws of self-examination serve to govern your everyday choices and decisions. Your life is an investment made by God. To fulfill your purpose, you have to shield and protect the divine investment and assignment you are carrying. Self-examination provides you with the opportunity to isolate in your life anything that could cause you to waste the precious assets in you.

The devil wants to get you to the state where you will be fruitless and useless. He has rendered so many Christians unproductive and useless to God by preoccupying them with things that don't have kingdom relevance. One way to protect your divine assignment, calling, or purpose is to undergird your life with a habit of self-examination.

2. Alarm

Without retreating into the closet of self-examination, certain alarm bells will not go off in your spirit, especially the alarm bells that erupt in areas of your life that need attention. When you begin the exercise of self-examination, it automatically causes certain alarm switches in your subconscious to activate and start buzzing. You will hear these in areas of your life where there are problems to address. This follows the same principle of the law of action and reaction.

Self-examination is the hand that opens the engine room of the subconscious soul and turns on the alarm when there is a fire raging in your heart. It's the hand that stubbornly rings the alarm bell until a dead conscience wakes up or the hardened soil of the heart softens. It's the hand that turns on the red light until the wagon of procrastination is halted. It's the hand that turns on the hazard light until action is taken to avert an imminent danger.

3. Manual

Self-examination could be said to be that self-written guide or manual that serves as your plan of action, reminder notice or alert. In the manual, you state lines or boundaries you cannot cross, things you cannot touch, places you cannot go, in order to preserve your integrity and anointing. In this manual, you list friends you cannot keep and associations you cannot belong to. Without guidelines for your life, you will fall for anything and everything.

You can run a race and miss the price if you don't follow the rules. In this era of preponderance of falsehood, you have to remind yourself to stick to the old-time religion continually. The manual of self-examination helps you to run by the rules. If you have not put down rules of engagement that I call the self-examination manual, it might be necessary to begin today. This is not legality; you are simply writing reminder notes or battle strategies for yourself and sticking them anywhere in the room of your mind and on the walls of your house.

The Bible is a divine manual. It has the roadmap to heaven. It has the master plan for victory. It is a manual you have to make your friend, as David testified in Psalm 119:11. It says,

**"Your word I have hidden in my heart,
That I might not sin against You."**

Written words serve as great guides. They also provide you with the opportunity to go back again and again to them when you are thirsty for more. If you go to some offices, you will see framed quotes of men and scriptures. Why do they proudly display these framed words on their walls? The reason is that they serve as messages to anyone who sets their eyes on them. Some of them are stored in our minds for a very long time. Write your quotes and mottos, especially those from the depths of your heart, or those borne out of the needs in your life, or those revealed to you by the Spirit of God. Stick them where you can see them; memorize them; live by them, and you will be a better person.

4. **Excavator**

Self–examination can serve as an excavator. It can dig deep into the dark chambers of your heart to unearth all you have buried there. Too many people walk around with ailments they are not aware of. Sometimes, it takes an explorative laparotomy in the surgical room, or some blood work in the laboratory, or a series of x-rays, to discover ailments. The same is true in the spiritual realm. Self-examination digs deep into your soul with its sharp teeth until it excavates the vestiges of the Adamic nature you have refused to deal with; vestiges that explain why you are hot-tempered or an emotional wreck or very impatient after over ten years of being a born-again Christian. These types of problems require sitting down and taking a closer look at your life before you can unravel their origins or come up with an offensive plan.

Beneath the paint job of an old house are many layers of coatings, each layer intended to conceal further the old blemishes of the house. On the contrary, there is no number of coatings or layers of paint, no matter how costly or beautiful, that can cover the sins that have darkened your heart.

Unfortunately, too many people spend all their lives trying so hard to cover their sins with many layers of nice clothes, expensive hats, and glowing eye goggles; or with lies upon lies, pride upon pride, and other worldly paints. Instead of these futile human effects, all you need is only one coating of the blood of Jesus. One coating of the blood of Jesus will outshine the millions of coatings you apply to cover your blemishes or hidden sins.

In our present world, we are too much in a hurry, so we have gotten hung up on quick fixes. This has driven many further into wearing many masks and living false lives. This is why they cave in or break into many hard pieces to piece together under any little pressure. Instead of going on with a cosmetic or artificial lifestyle, take time to meditate and think through your life's purpose and the direction your life is heading to. This book is intended to slow you down and help you refocus and re-evaluate your life in order to solve your present challenges or avert future problems.

5. Roadmap

The simple reason smart people travel with roadmaps or navigators is to make sure they don't get lost. Why then do you travel along the highways and byways of life without one? Self-examination can serve as a good roadmap for the right direction to follow when you come to a crossroads. It can serve as a road sign pointing you to the things you need to address; or to the areas of your life that need the touch of God.

Roadmaps or navigators do highlight problem areas on the way to help you avoid delays or disasters. The roadmap of self-examination will not do any less for you. It's meant to keep you safe and to help you navigate through challenging areas of life. Take it with you as you travel through life every day.

6. Starting point

Self-examination serves as the starting point for an overhaul project, be it a soured relationship or eating habits; when you are at a loss, what to do is to start with self-examination. Before a builder builds a house, he must first weed and prepare the ground and its surroundings. Employ the service of self-examination to begin your future projects, be it marriage, moving to another city, or changing job.

Self-examination is the first step you have to take to get yourself moving in the right direction, be it climbing out of a pit; or ascending from a steep declivity where you have been held captive by circumstances or aberrant habits. It could also serve as the starting line for the race of discovery or recovery.

7. Guardrails

Self–examination can serve as guardrails to keep you from straying away from the right course. Creating boundaries can help keep you in check or stop you from wandering away from your assignment or purpose. Too many Christians are copycats. If they see another Christian going to a movie theater, they immediately plan to also go to a movie. While going to a movie theater may not be bad, it may be an unnecessary weight for you. You may have a higher calling that demands a higher consecration; so, don't copy what others are doing. Create guide rails for yourself based on the level of your divine assignment. Listen to the Holy Spirit. Pay attention to His leading and not what others are doing.

8. Surgical blade

It serves as a lancet to nip any budding sin or as a knife to cut down any wild tree growing in the landscape of your heart. Your heart is precious and should be jealously guarded. Use whatever you can, including the trimming knife of self-examination, to shield and protect it. Trim your life daily; weed it daily, and you will transform yourself into someone your family, friends, pastor, and other Christians would be proud of.

9. Cleanser

If you turn on the flushing water of self-examination every day, it will flush out the debris you have gathered from your journey so far. We are exposed to too many things every day, some of which we absorb and store in our subconscious. If you don't shower every day, you will leave a trail of bad smell everywhere you go. But when you take your shower every day, you will look and smell good.

Some people, especially teenagers, have the habit of not washing their plates after eating. When they go to wash them, they discover they have a much more challenging task to deal with because the leftover food has hardened. That's what we do with our lives. We leave bad habits to harden before we begin to address them. Sometimes the battle to free ourselves after the sinful habits have hardened can go on forever. It's, therefore, wise to flush out any debris of sin before it hardens in your heart.

10. Floodlight

If you don't leave the lights on at night, you may stub your toe, which can be very painful. Too many times, we put off changing a dead light bulb. It's only when we have hurt ourselves several times that we finally get to it. A lifestyle of self-examination makes sure that you attend to your daily problems. It opens your eyes to see the danger of procrastination. It shines a bright light on the problem you are dealing with, making it harder for you to ignore for a long time.

If your driveway is dark, someone can hide there and possibly pose a danger to you. Self-examination lights up the dark corners of your heart for you to see anything hiding in it. With the floodlight of self-examination, everything hiding in your life will be exposed.

11. Other purposes

There are too many merits of the laws of self-examination to enumerate. Among other reasons, self-examination serves to make you aware of your environment and your challenges. It draws the curtain of the darkrooms of your heart for you to see what you couldn't see in darkness; it wakes you up from slumber and serves as a deterrent from repeating old mistakes. It helps you to be sensitive spiritually. It helps you to walk in the path of righteousness and purity, preserving you for the appearing of the Lord. 1 John 3:3 says, **"And everyone who has this hope in Him purifies himself, just as He is pure."**

Anyone who has this hope does not live carelessly. He constantly examines himself, making sure he is always on the right path. According to 2 Corinthians 13:5, you should continuously **"Examine yourselves *as to* whether you are in the faith. Test yourselves. Do you not know yourselves that Jesus Christ is in you? —unless indeed you are disqualified."**

THE DEMANDS OF SELF-EXAMINATION

Self-examination places certain demands on your shoulders. For it to be effective and produce a noticeable change in your life, you have to live up to its demands.

1. Moral strength:

Self-examination demands the moral strength and readiness to follow instructions and corrections. It demands the moral strength to be honest, humble enough to accept responsibilities, and act accordingly.

2. **Scheduling**

It demands planning and time allocation. If you don't schedule it, you may never form the habit of doing it. Let your plan be attainable. Make room also for some flexibility but don't fail to make it a daily exercise. Don't put it off, or you will be caught in the costly net of procrastination.

3. **Journaling**

It demands having a notebook and a pen. Journaling will help you have a structure in your life. It simplifies things for you. Habakkuk 2:2 says,

"…Write the vision
And make *it* plain on tablets,
That he may run who reads it."

Writing daily in your journal offers you a world of great possibilities of exploring the inner chambers of your thoughts and expressing them in such ways that will be easy to remember. It's a wonderful way to capture the most important parts of your life beautifully.

Today in my journal, I wrote down my scriptures of the day, 1 Peter 3:3-4:

"Do not let your adornment be *merely* outward—
arranging the hair, wearing gold, or putting
on *fine* apparel—rather *let it be* the hidden person of the heart, with the incorruptible *beauty* of a gentle and quiet

spirit, which is very precious in the sight of God."

These two verses will serve as "a lamp to my feet and my path" for the rest of the day. They will serve as the yardsticks to measure my actions and thoughts for the day. Any person who invests a scriptural verse in his life every day, in ten years, it can be said

"He shall be like a tree
Planted by the rivers of water,
That brings forth its fruit in its season,
Whose leaf also shall not wither;
And whatever he does shall prosper" (Psalm 1:3).

Multitude of questions and answers

Self-examination demands you ask yourself hard questions. One question a day may suffice. If you can answer it sincerely, you would have laid another brick in your foundation, making you better suited to withstand adversity. Those who avoid the important questions of today would be forced to answer them when they are least prepared.

Questions are very revealing. They have a way of bringing hidden things to the surface. It's an excellent way to start the journey of self-discovery. When you meet someone for the first time, one of the best ways to begin to acquaint yourself with him or her is to start with a question. *How are you?* Or, *what's your name?* In the same vein, real spiritual growth and discovery begin when you start asking questions about your purpose, destiny, character, or faithfulness to your divine assignment. A question a day will save you from a million mistakes and heartaches. In the multitude of questions, there is safety and no scarcity of knowledge and truth.

Here are some questions that may help you to start your day.

- Who is in charge today, the Spirit (of God) or my flesh?
- What are the things I am still struggling with? How can I address them today?
- What is the Word for the day? Do I have a scripture handy as my weapon of offense and defense?
- Where is my focus today? Is it on the size of my mountain or on the greatness of my God?
- Can I truly say that I am a good father, or husband, or wife, or neighbor, or friend, or sister, or brother, or uncle, or aunty, or co-worker, or boss, or leader, as the case maybe? What can I do today to improve?
- What can I do today that will draw me closer to God?
- What can I do today to put a smile on someone's face or make the burden of someone lighter?
- How much time did I spend being thankful today?
- How did I address my greatest challenge of the day? Would God be proud or ashamed of me because of the way I handled my problems today?

- How did I respond to those who were unfriendly to me today? Was there a show of humility or pride? Was there a show of love or hatred? Was there a show of respect or disrespect?
- Today, did I intentionally misrepresent anyone or anything?
- Is there resentment and unforgiveness in my heart?
- How easy is it for me to make excuses for my failures, or how easy is it for me to blame others?
- What sin is driving a wedge between God and me? Is it not time to surrender it to God?
- What is that idol in my life that is hard to let go of? Is it really worth losing my soul eternally for?
- How many times have I resisted the Holy Spirit's instruction to totally surrender every area of my life to Him so that God can use me for His glory?
- How many times has God beckoned on me to draw closer to Him, and I resisted or flatly refused? How long will I continue to be a rebel?
- What is that thing in my life that makes me feel unworthy to be used by God? What am I going to do about it today?
- What is that thing that weakens my strength and makes

me unable to resist certain temptations?

- What is that thing that ties my hands, making me a captive to sin?
- Can God trust me? How dependable am I?
- What do I lay much emphasis on every day? Is it my physical appearance or the acquisition of wealth? Do I know how to balance my physical with my spiritual wellbeing?
- What keeps me awake at night? Is it my dwindling bank account or my anemic spiritual life?

The more questions you ask, the more you discover about yourself, and the more equipped you are to deal with your everyday challenges.

4. Have another Eye

Self-examination demands you have someone to keep an eye on you, someone to be accountable to. Let it be someone bold enough to tell you the truth. Your best friends are not those who let you do whatever you like but those who politely but firmly reprimand and correct you when you do something wrong. Getting an honest and constructive feedback from true friends or family members or your mentor on how you are doing is a healthy lifestyle. A life without boundaries is a life headed for disaster. A life without checks and balances is headed for shame and disgrace.

5. Resources

Self-examination demands the habit of reading your Bible, the habit of reading good inspirational books, biographies of great men, and other informative books. Build a library of great books and attend life-changing conferences. Invest your time and money in things that will improve the quality of your life. By so doing, you will acquire great knowledge and wisdom that may help re-structure your life and make it more productive.

Many people are quick to invest in ornaments and the latest fashions and gadgets but are slow to invest in resources that can take them where their precious stones and external adornments cannot take them. What you spend your money on reveals what your values are.

6. Measuring your progress

Self-examination demands you have a way of measuring your progress. Any work or labor that the correct standards of measurement cannot measure will be hard to build on or maximized. Measure your progress regularly. It will help you to make the necessary adjustments.

THE CONSEQUENCES OF BREAKING THE LAWS

Breaking the laws of self-examination has far-reaching consequences than most laws you may be familiar with. Let's take a look at some of the consequences.

1. MORAL CONSEQUENCES

When the hedge of self-examination is eroded, moral boundaries will also be eroded. Moral turpitude is costly to a society and to individuals who perpetuate them. It destroys careers, marriages, and even lives. It can reduce noble dreams, worthy goals, and thrones to ashes.

If there is an area the Christian should pay more attention it is the area of morality. Immorality is the order of the day and a tool the devil has capitalized on in his deception schemes, dragging thousands daily to hell. Everywhere you turn, the eye is bombarded and assaulted with a toxic dose of immorality. Make no mistake about it; if you don't have a solid everyday battle plan, you may not survive the barrage of satanic attacks and onslaught against your morality. Without setting boundaries, you stand a chance of being a casualty of the fast-rolling caravan of immorality the devil uses to run over unguarded people from generation to generation.

The Bible says,

"Be sober, be vigilant; because your adversary the devil walks about like a roaring lion, seeking whom he may devour. Resist him, steadfast in the faith, knowing that the same sufferings are experienced by your brotherhood in the world" (1 Peter 5:8-9).

A life without self-examination is a reckless life. The prodigal son tried living such a life in a foreign land, but after a while, he discovered there is more to life than meets the eye. Life dealt with him so badly that he found himself in the gutters begging for pig's leftovers.

"But when he had spent all, there arose a severe famine in that land, and he began to be in want. Then he went and joined himself to a citizen of that country, and he sent him into his fields to feed swine. And he would gladly have filled his stomach with the pods that the swine ate, and no one gave him *anything*" (Luke 15:14-16).

A life of self-examination will save you a lot of the heartaches and pains that the prodigal son went through because he chose to live a life without checks and balances. The truth is that human beings are capable of being extremely evil. At one time in the history of mankind, God regretted creating man because of man's constant evil works.

"Then the LORD saw that the wickedness of
man *was* great in the earth and *that* every intent of the
thoughts of his heart *was* only
evil continually. And the LORD was sorry that He had made man on the earth, and He was grieved in His heart" (Genesis 6: 5-6).

As a bad child breaks the heart of his father or mother, so a morally decadent person or society breaks the heart of God. Every day, your life is adding to the beauty of the world or to its ugliness. Every day your life brings glory to God or brings shame to the church that Jesus died for. Every day we are morally accountable to God.

HISTORICAL CONSEQUENCES

Too many people in history laid down wrong and false foundations that have been misleading younger generations. They include politicians, clergies, traditional leaders, newscasters, professors, parents, and many others. They laid on hilltops and parchments, corrosive historical precedents, footprints that have pointed the world in the wrong direction. Some of them broke every law in the book and threw caution to the winds in their quest for fame, money, and authority.

a. Politicians

Everywhere you go, you will find good and bad politicians; good and bad leaders. In Africa, most politicians see their office as the opportunity to amass wealth. As soon as they force themselves into office, within few months, they become millionaires and billionaires. They simply loot what their predecessors left. If there is not enough left in the government coffers to steal, they take huge loans from the Western world at a very high-interest rate and turn around and share each of the loans among themselves. With the stolen money in their pockets, they become scoundrels, gods, and 'mighty' personalities. People begin to worship them, and if you don't, they oppress you.

This has made political offices the most lucrative jobs in Africa and the envy and aspirations of younger generations. And since these politicians get away with their stolen money, the culture of corruption has become the order of the day in the African society.

Corrupt politicians seem to have no conscience. The African roads are bad, paved with the blood of innocent travelers who die daily maneuvering dangerous potholes, not paved with tar. What is more? Electricity is a luxury rare to find both in small and big cities in Africa. In the 21st century Africa, good hospitals are blue moons, and good running water is non-existent. There are no basic amenities of life in 21st century Africa!

With the looted money, the politicians buy houses in several overseas countries, send their children and concubines abroad, and set up fat bank accounts for them. Most of them at death have billions of dollars in foreign banks that cannot be recovered. All these go on from one regime to another in most African countries in the face of the very low GDP and very high unemployment rates the continent is battling with. The debts most African countries owe World Bank, and other foreign nations may take over two hundred years to pay back.

These heartless leaders have mortgaged their unborn children's future and the future of their countries with debts they have no means of paying back. The amount of money left in foreign banks by dead African politicians is big enough to put every African to work. Unfortunately, most of these monies are unrecoverable. Hence Africans are escaping their shores in hordes in search of livelihood in foreign countries. These foreign countries are ironically partly sustained by the monies looted by Africa's dead and living politicians.

Historically, politicians on African soil have laid bad

precedence, and the younger generations are towing the same path. It's important to note that most of Africa's corruptions are masterminded by foreign countries that see a decadent society as a gold mine.

Be careful about the foundation you are laying. With a sustained lifestyle of self-examination, you can keep yourself unspotted and unpolluted, even amid a perverse generation from whom we are called to separate ourselves.

The Bible says,

"Do all things without complaining and disputing, that you may become blameless and harmless, children of God without fault in the midst of a crooked and perverse generation, among whom you shine as lights in the world, holding fast the word of life, so that I may rejoice in the day of Christ that I have not run in vain or labored in vain" (Philippians 2:14-16).

A daily life of self-examination will help ensure that you will not run or labor in vain for the Lord. I have been a born-again Christian for over forty-five years, and many times, I have reminded myself to do everything I can to make sure all these years of serving the Lord will not be in vain.

b. Fashion Designers

Many people ignore what they wear in terms of its moral fitness and significance as long as it is in vogue. With self-examination, you will be able to take a closer look at most of what you do, including the clothes you wear every day. When a woman wears revealing clothes, she leaves a bad impression in the hearts of morally upright observers. Not every fashion is appropriate for the Christian. 1 Timothy 4:12 calls us to live an exemplary life. It says,

"Let no one despise your youth, but be an example to the believers in word, in conduct, in love, in spirit, in faith, in purity."

As a fashion designer, are you releasing designs that are acceptable to God, or are you creating styles that leave women half naked just to make money? What foundation are you laying? What footprints are you leaving? Self-examination will help you to answer these questions. Any clothing design you cannot proudly wear before God if He appears in Person before you are meant for the gutter. That should be the litmus test.

c. Pastors

Pastors have a big podium, the pulpit. Africans are very religious people and literally believe everything that comes from the pulpit. That's why it's easy to manipulate and control them. For this reason, pastors have to be very careful with the seed they are sowing in people's hearts. Search your heart daily. Examine your motive constantly. Let your prayer every day be,

"Examine me, O LORD, and prove me;
Try my mind and my heart.
For Your lovingkindness *is* before my eyes,
And I have walked in Your truth" (Psalms 26:2-3).

We live in an age that sees many wolves taking to the pulpits, deceiving the uninformed and gullible with their diet of lies, diction of poetry, and great oratory that lack the truth of the gospel of Jesus. But it's important to note that there are still significant remnants of pastors who proclaim the whole counsel of the risen Savior, Jesus Christ, who make no apologies for the sound gospel they preach and teach as they patiently wait for the soon coming King.

d. Parents

Children, most times, tow the footsteps of their parents. Many children with fathers or mothers as medical doctors, lawyers, or engineers end up with their parents' careers. No one can shape the destiny or life of a child more than his or her parents. What foundation are you laying for your children? Do you consider them when you make certain decisions?

Stop every day in front of the mirror and see the face of who you are replicating or patterning your children after. If you don't like what you are seeing, then do something about it before it is too late. After about the age of ten, it becomes harder to change the behavior of a child. If you plant a wrong seed in them in their formative years, the harm is already done. Take time to plant the right seed in them from today, no matter the price you have to pay. It will be worth it.

e. Other leaders

Every leader wields a lot of power, from presidents of nations and corporations to traditional rulers and mayors. Without a conscience undergirded by a lifestyle of self-examination, they can wrongly influence the world. Bad leaders replicate bad leaders, and good leaders replicate good leaders. That is why we should never vote a bad leader into office. Unfortunately, in Africa, they force their way into office by any means.

What footprints are you leaving behind you? History will judge you, and even if you escape the judgment of men, you will never escape the judgment of God. Romans 14:12 says, **"So then each of us shall give account of himself to God."**

CHAPTER THREE

THE FIRST LAW OF SELF-EXAMINATION

I call to remembrance my song in the night; I meditate within my heart,
And my spirit makes diligent search.
– Psalm 77:6

The First Law of Self-Examination: ***Examine yourself before you examine others.***

Too often, we are so focused on others' faults that we become blind to our own faults. Many times, when a good message is being preached in the church by a pastor, you are busy wishing your spouse or friend were there to hear what the pastor is saying. In your mind, they are the ones that need the message, not you. That is a pointer that pride has so clouded your eyes and mind that you can't see your sins; all you see are the sins of others.

Better than binoculars

I once owned a pair of powerful binoculars. With it, I could see far into distances that I couldn't see before. It was an exciting vacation accessory. If I focus it on distant trees, it's possible to see birds hopping from one branch to another. It had the ability to reveal to me things hidden from me by distance. That's the beauty of binoculars.

Self-examination can give you the advantage my binoculars gave me and even more. If you use the binoculars of self-examination, you could see things buried deep in your life that you wouldn't see ordinarily. It gives you the advantage of identifying your hidden sins before they have the chance to destroy your career, your marriage, or your life. Without the binoculars of self-examination, it will be harder to see your shortcomings but easier to see those of others.

There are people whose motto is "Follow my words and not my actions." Such people are everywhere, from politics to pulpits. Before you ask your neighbor to remove the blemish in his eyes, first remove yours; otherwise, you make yourself a hypocrite. That might sound like an archaic word, but if you would use the binoculars of self-examination to take a closer look at your life, you may be surprised how well that word describes you. Many people hide behind a mask, pretending to be what they are not.

In every generation, there are leaders who do not command much respect and influence because of their deplorable lifestyles, so they resort to the use of force to earn their respect. In the end, all they succeed in doing is instilling fear in the heart of people but may never earn the respect of these people unless they address the issues that made them monsters. You cannot lead by example if you have no room in your heart for self-examination. Such a leader could be described as a physician in need of a physician. Matthew 7:3 asks a very important question, **"And why do you look at the speck in your brother's eye, but do not consider the plank in your own eye?"**

In the words of Nelson Mandela, **"One of the things I learned when I was negotiating was that until I changed myself, I could not change others."** You can fool yourself as long as you want, but you cannot fool the world forever. It's a matter of time your true face would be unveiled. There is always a day of reckoning, a day of accountability that no mortal will escape.

Your life is a book

As the coming of Christ draws near, the world is becoming darker and darker. Every day, it's harder to separate the wheat from the tares or the believer from the unbeliever. The margin has been blurred. The world needs people who lead by example, leaders whose light can overpower the surging darkness.

In one of my poems, I wrote:

If you were a book, everyone would read
in the pages of your life,
would the grieving find solace,
the wounded find healing
and the hopeless find hope?

Would your testimonies bestow

courage to the fearful,
joy to the sorrowful,
freedom to the captive,
and strength to the weak?

At the turn of each page,
would the story of your life
stir up faith in the heart of the faithless?
Would the face of the weary
glow with confidence?
Would someone whose dreams has died
become pregnant with new dreams?
When the last page of your life is read,
would your life be a refreshing ointment,
a precious ornament of hope,
a treasure proudly displayed
on the shelves of people's minds?

Or would it be another book
quickly tossed away
like an old musty loaf of bread?

When the last page of the book of your life is read, I pray you would not be another soul quickly tossed into the fire of hell to burn; instead, your life would be a glorious testimony provoking people to bear the cross of the gospel of Christ with unshakable faith.

Unrepentant sin

The story of King David and Nathan drives home the important point of self-examination in leadership. Let us take a close look at it.

"Then the LORD sent Nathan to David. And he came to him, and said to him: "There were two men in one city, one rich and the other poor. The rich *man* had exceedingly many flocks and herds. But the poor *man* had nothing, except one little ewe lamb which he had bought and nourished; and it grew up together with him and with his children. It ate of his own food and drank from his own cup and lay in his bosom; and it was like a daughter to him. And a traveler came to the rich man, who refused to take from his own flock and from his own herd to prepare one for the wayfaring man who had come to him; but he took the poor man's lamb and prepared it for the man who had come to him."

So David's anger was greatly aroused against the man, and he said to Nathan, "*As* the LORD lives, the man who has done this shall surely die! And he shall restore fourfold for the lamb, because he did this thing and because he had no pity."

Then Nathan said to David, "You *are* the man! ...."

- 2 Samuel 12: 1-7

David was a great and respected leader, but he failed to lead by example at this point in his life. We can hide from a man, but we cannot hide from God. When we are stubborn or wicked, He knows how to bring us to our knees. Too many times, we fail to realize that it's better to stand before the mirror of self-examination and take a look into our lives and deal with what it reveals to us before a Nathan in our job or family or church exposes us.

David was supposed to be heading the army of Israel at the time in question; instead, he decided to stay home. When you substitute your assignment for pleasure or leisure, you could easily be distracted, and before you knew it, you would be in trouble.

Do not delegate what God has instructed you to do. Do not succumb to fear or laziness when you are needed on the battlefield. It's a generally accepted fact that the time in which a nation, a church, or family is facing difficulty is not the time for a leader to be missing in action. It's like sleeping when your house is on fire.

2 Samuel 11:1 says, **"It happened in the spring of the year, at the time when kings go out *to battle,* that David sent Joab and his servants with him, and all Israel; and they destroyed the people of Ammon and besieged Rabbah. But David remained at Jerusalem."**

It was springtime. Maybe the flowers were blossoming, and their fragrance wafted into the nostrils of David while he was lying on his bed. 2 Samuel 11:2 says, **"Then it happened one evening that David arose from his bed and walked on the roof of the king's house. And from the roof, he saw a woman bathing, and the woman *was* very beautiful to behold."** How many times have we used our prayer time to make unimportant phone calls, watch TV, or engage in leisurely activity?

Standing at a vantage point of his balcony to feed his eyes, David saw Bathsheba's nakedness, and his trouble began. Suddenly lust gripped him. Using his kingly power, he eventually did the bidding of his flesh by sleeping with her. When the woman got pregnant from their union, he sought for a cover-up. That culminated in sending Uriah, Bathsheba's husband, to the battlefield's frontline, which led to his death. David did not stop there. After Uriah's death, David married Bathsheba and even fathered a son with her.

2 Samuel 11:27 says, **"...But the thing David had done displeased the Lord."**

How did David not see his sins before Nathan came? God must have waited for a while for him to repent but to no avail. He had to send Nathan to him. It took Nathan's visit to bring David to the place of remorse and repentance. 2 Samuel 12:13 says, **"So David said to Nathan, "I have sinned against the LORD."**

How many times have we lived with unrepentant sins? Certainly, David is not the only one who has done this. Some men have had affairs with a Bathsheba but never confessed their sins and repented before their maker; some have the secret habit of watching pornography; some have defiled their housemaids and kept it a secret. Some pastors have even slept with some of their female church members and still preach every Wednesday and Sunday with unconfessed sins. There is more to a person than meets the eye.

These days, even when God sends a Nathan to some

Christians, they would call him a false prophet. Many have become so defiant; their consciences are seared. They have become brazenly evil-doing all kinds of things in the house of God. I believe a life of daily self-examination would have served David very well at a time like this. It would have been the first self-help manual he would have grabbed from the shelf of heart and read every page thoroughly. It would have brought him to his knees before Nathan came.

The little price you and I will pay for the structured lifestyle of self-examination is nothing compared to the value it bestows on us. Even if it demands you change your career, or walk away from a friend with bad influence, or turn your back to a food you love so much, in the end, the sacrifice would be worth it.

Self-examination is an invaluable asset. It's a powerful tool that can systematically dismantle the strong hedges of a bad habit; it's a seemingly uncomplicated implement that can uproot the stubborn roots of besetting sins. Without a lifestyle of self-examination, your life is at risk. You could easily overlook little pitfalls along the way and may even stumble over them and fall. But with a lifestyle of self-examination, your eyes are always open and alert, watching for any hurdle along the way.

No matter how little time you give to self-examination each day, you will have great results. That's how potent the daily pill of self-examination can be. The size of its pill does not degrade its power. No matter how small it is, if taken consistently, it can lift you out of the quagmire of habits that are incinerating your soul day by day. It's a little knife that has the power to cut the strong ropes that have restrained your hands; the little flame that can rekindle the fire of your old love for God.

If you take a little time out of your busy schedule to examine your life each day, you will see the difference it will make in your life in a short period. Wise people don't wait until their trash starts stinking before they take it out. Don't wait until your trash becomes too heavy for you to deal with. Deal with your sin before it deals with you. Take it to the cross and leave it there!

In the words of Nelson Mandela, **"As we let our own light shine, we unconsciously give other people permission to do the same."** That's what a great leader does. He leads by example.

CHAPTER FOUR

THE SECOND LAW OF SELF-EXAMINATION

Surely, after my turning, I repented; And after I was instructed, I struck myself on the thigh;
I was ashamed, yes, even humiliated, Because I bore the reproach of my youth.'
– Jeremiah 31:19.

The second law of self-examination: ***Without humility, there will be no visibility.***

When you are driving down a road with poor visibility, you drive with caution. In some countries, you are required to turn on your headlamps at such times to make your vehicle more visible to other motorists. Also, when you have to drive in the rain, you turn on your wiper to keep the rain off your windscreen or windshield; otherwise, it will be impossible for you to see through it. This means that there are things that can hinder visibility. This is true both in the physical and spiritual realms.

Poor visibility

Pride is one of such things that can hinder your spiritual visibility. If you wear the robe of pride, it will hinder your moral vision. With poor visibility, you cannot decipher your ailments. Such people always want to be the only ones to be seen or heard. That is why pride is a great obstacle to spiritual growth. While others are busy praising God in the church, the proud is busy worrying about his looks; while others are coming to the altar to repent or to rededicate their lives to the Lord, the proud is busy hiding his sins as hard as he can; pretending to be what he is not.

Pride has ruined the ministries of many great men of God. Some of them have stolen the glory of God in their churches, in their bid for human worship and praise, being easily offended when addressed as pastors instead of Daddies and Mommies, sometimes wielding authorities akin to dictatorship. What they forgot is that **"God resists the proud, but gives grace to the humble" (James 4:6).**

Pride is a dangerous path to travel, a path that leads to self-worship and eventually self-destruction. It closes the door to self-examination. It clogs the ear so that it cannot hear. It blindfolds the eyes so that it cannot see. It's something to closely watch so that it does not creep into your life and ruin your life and ministry before you realize it.

When pride possesses a heart, it manifests at all times. It's a solid captive chain. Most times, those under the captive chain of pride are unaware of their problems. They are one of the most complicated people to preach. They always assume they know more than the preacher. In a crowd, they believe they are better than everyone else. In the classroom or office, they are the loudest.

I remember asking a lady who relocated to Atlanta about a medical doctor I knew who lived in the state she just left. This lady could be described as one of those conservative and seemingly disciplined women. She surprised me by volunteering information I never asked for when she described the doctor as the most arrogant man she had ever known. It threw me aback. From my little interaction with this doctor, he presented himself as a simple and humble person. So, what drove this lady to such a conclusion about him? What did she see in his life that he was not seeing?

What do people see in our lives that we don't see? This very important question is why we ought to pray to God every day to show us the hidden sins in our lives. We ought to pray every day like Job, **"How many are my iniquities and sins? Make me know my transgression and my sin" (Job 12:23).**

Great visibility with humility

Dealing with pride is not an easy thing. But if you make self-examination the first page you turn to when you are ready to read the old, unattractive book of humility, you will deal a big blow to pride.

Humility is not subjecting yourself to mediocrity but avoiding making yourself the subject matter every time. Self-examination will methodically unknot the thread that has woven pride deep into the fabrics of your heart. It will open the secret doors in your heart for you to see the hidden dungeons of pride. It's the medicine, when taken daily or regularly, that will slowly loosen the years of hardened sewage of pride, making it easy for the Holy Spirit to flush it out.

Self-examination is to humility what a hoe is to a farmer. It helps the farmer, among other things, to weed his farm in order to save his crops. Self-examination is to the heart what radar is to an aircraft. It sends warning signals to it when it detects any danger in its vicinity. Self-examination is to the heart what a rudder is to a ship. It helps to steer it out of danger. But it's only useful when we put it to work.

If you avail yourself of the powerful self-examination tool, you will be ashamed to wear the filthy garment of pride even for one day. The garment of humility will shield you from God's anger, but the garment of pride will draw His wrath. The garment of humility will bring out the beauty of God in you, but the garment of pride will make you a monster.

Does pride soil your garment? Are you always talking about yourself? Do you always want to be seen and heard? Are you constantly seeking men's applause and praise? Do you give so that men will praise you? What is the motive behind your actions? Can you stand before God and boldly declare that you are a man or woman devoid of pride?

1 Corinthians 11:31sums it up. **"For if we would judge ourselves, we would not be judged."** If indeed we examine

our lives today, we will evade the judgment of tomorrow.

CHAPTER FIVE

THE THIRD LAW OF SELF-EXAMINATION

Your word is a lamp to my feet
And a light to my path.
– Psalm 119:105

The third law of self-examination: ***To avoid looking at the mirror is to avoid telling yourself the truth.***

Mirror is one of the most powerful tools for self-examination. With the mirror, you can see any blemish on your face. The mirror tells you the truth. It does not sugarcoat a defect on your face. So, when you fail to look at the mirror, you will never see the need to get help or do something about your situation.

More than likely, before you leave the house, you always take a good look at yourself in the mirror. You want to be sure you look good. You want to make sure there is nothing on your face that can cause you embarrassment. If you use the mirror daily because you cannot afford to expose yourself to public ridicule and embarrassment, why then do you neglect the mirror of self-examination? When was the last time you sat down and took a closer look at your daily habits or lifestyle?

The Bible is an invaluable mirror. It was given to humanity by God to show us the state of our hearts and point us in the right direction. If you spend a little time every day before this infallible and unblemished mirror, it will automatically alter your life. It will transform you from a sinner to a saint, from a prisoner of bad habits to a Christian walking daily in victory. Over time, your life will bloom with righteousness and fruitfulness. The book of Psalms tells us that

"Blessed *is* the man
Who walks not in the counsel of the ungodly,
Nor stands in the path of sinners,
Nor sits in the seat of the scornful;
But his delight *is* in the law of the LORD,
And in His law, he meditates day and night.
He shall be like a tree
Planted by the rivers of water,
That brings forth its fruit in its season,
Whose leaf also shall not wither;
And whatever he does shall prosper."

- Psalms 1:1-3

Obviously, you cannot remain the same if you spend time looking into this Mirror or law of God. It has a cleansing, a healing, and a liberating power. It has an inspiring, purifying, and edifying power.

ETERNAL VALUES

It's important to distinguish between the physical breakable mirrors that we sometimes hang on our rooms' walls from the Mirror of life, which is the incorruptible Word of God, the Bible. The physical mirror has temporary values, but the Mirror of life has eternal values. Here are a few things of eternal value the Bible will show you.

1. It will show you the hidden things of the heart

The Mirror will show you where there is a crack on the wall of your heart. It will show you the covetousness, jealousy, envy, and many other secret sins in your heart. It will show the river of pride overflowing the banks of your heart like a mighty ocean and flooding the shores of your life, ruining your character and a lot of your relationships.

When you don't look into the Word of God, you will begin to be attracted to the idols of the world. What are the idols in your life, the idols you have bartered for the place of God? Too many times, we substitute God with idols and knowingly or unknowingly enter into contracts with them. Your church can be your idol if you don't surrender it to the Lordship of Christ; your job can be your idol if you make it the most important thing in your life. Some even go as far as entrusting their lives to a piece of charm and proudly wear it on their fingers or around their waists. What an utter risk to take!

I remember the day I extricated two young men, with the help of others, from their badly damaged car and rushed them to a nearby hospital. They were traveling in a Volvo sedan and had a head-on collision with a bus carrying over twenty passengers. The accident happened a few miles to Owerri, a city in southeastern Nigeria. It was a bad collision. What struck me most was the fact that one of the men had a charm around his waist. When I visited the hospital the next day to check on them, I was told he did not make it. He died despite the charm around his waist. Sadly, his idol couldn't save him.

If you must keep away from anything, don't keep away from the Mirror of life even for one day, more so as the day of the Lord's coming is drawing near. Joel 2:1 says,

"Blow the trumpet in Zion,
And sound an alarm in My holy mountain!
Let all the inhabitants of the land tremble;
For the day of the LORD is coming,
For it is at hand: ..."

There are two magnetic forces we are subject to, the divine magnetic force that pulls us towards God and the magnetic force of the world that pulls us away from God. The day you stop feeding your soul with the rejuvenating Word of God, its magnetic force starts loosening its hold on you, and the magnetic force of the world starts gaining its hold on you. It can be a subtle transition. When you see your spouse gradually turning into a different person, it could be he is slowly walking away from God or, unknowingly, walking into the seductive holds of the world. Don't keep quiet in such situations. Engage in the spiritual battle needed to pull him back from the stronghold of the world. Engage in prayers; increase your loving attitude towards him/her; engage in a combatant rebuilding of the family altar. Matthew 11:12 says, **"And from the days of John the Baptist until now the kingdom of heaven suffers violence, and the violent take it by force."**

2. It will show you the secret of passing the tests of life

In life, tests are unavoidable. They reveal who you are. Without them, you may never discover what you know and what you don't know; without them, you may never discover what you can do and what you can't do. Tests come in different shapes and sizes. Sometimes it comes as a trial or tribulation, and sometimes it comes as a job promotion or a huge financial blessing. Oh yes, a financial blessing can be a test.

I recall the story my wife told me about one very seemingly nice and devoted brother everybody in her former church loved and respected. One faithful day he got a huge financial blessing, and the next Sunday, nobody saw him in church. As soon as he got the financial blessing, he walked away from God and walked into the world with open arms. Within the next few years, the news came to the church that he was dead. The news broke the heart of everyone. As painful as his death was, the fact remains that he failed the test of a little promotion.

Life is a school that begins at infancy. In this private citadel of learning, you acquire the skills for warfare and brace up for the unforeseen circumstances of life. Those who excel in this tutelage always excel in life. One of the greatest tools God gave man to learn the secret of warfare is, again, the Bible. For this reason, Joshua 1:8 advises that,

"This Book of the Law shall not depart from your mouth, but you shall meditate in it day and night, that you may observe to do according to all that is written in it. For then you will make your way prosperous, and then you will have good success."

Winning does not just happen. When you desire to be the best, you will constantly evaluate and re-evaluate yourself; you will constantly stand in front of the mirror to see your life's present state. Every winner has a penchant for skill acquisition and self-improvement. Things are not to be left to chance. Proverbs 22:29 says,

"Do you see a man *who* excels in his work?
He will stand before kings;
He will not stand before unknown *men*."

Do you have a winner's lifestyle? In the last twenty hours, how much time did you spend on self-improvement? How much money have you invested in things that will improve your skills and spiritual life in the last three months? One of the greatest problems of our age is that many people have become too superficial and artificial. They lack the patience to invest in quality, so they resort to make-belief and whitewashed marketing style that easily exposes their lack of root and authenticity when the wind of adversity blows.

What is your foremost heart cry today? Maybe, "God, bless me with a big house, a beautiful car, a coffer full of money, a lucrative job or business?" These are wonderful things, but they should not be the foremost things in your life. If you embrace God's daily prescription of the Mirror of life for your ailments, your roots will be deep, and you will stand in the times of adversity; you will stand when others are falling to pornography, bribery and corruption, and to other gods of this world.

3. It will show you the source of wisdom

With wisdom in the driver's seat, you will never be lost in your journey. Before you accelerate your car across the dangerous bridges of life, take the advice of Proverb 4:7,

"Wisdom *is* the principal thing;
***Therefore* get wisdom.**
And in all your getting, get understanding."

No matter what project you want to embark on, don't get started without seeking first the wisdom of God. Ecclesiastes 7:12 says, **"For wisdom *is* a defense *as* money *is* a defense, But the excellence of knowledge *is that* wisdom gives life to those who have it."**

Many fail in life because they lack the wisdom to excel. Wisdom is the wheel that turns the wagon of life down the road of success. It has the power to transform barren land into a beautiful and fruitful landscape when it comes from the refreshing well of the Word of God. Men's wisdom and philosophies are no match to the wisdom of the all-knowing, all-powerful, infallible God! Wise men seek refuge in God and

His Word; fools seek refuge in their wealth, titles, and other accomplishments.

4. It will show you the path to a disciplined life

A disciplined life is the envy of everyone, yet it's elusive to many. The reason is that many do not stop to find out the root cause of their indiscipline. The root cause is not due to your race, or nationality like some racially minded people want the world to believe. The root cause is because of the Adamic or fallen nature of man. This nature is inherent in every man or woman, regardless of your skin color. It's that fallen nature that drives a man to sin, and the only remedy for man is to take the prescription of his Maker, and that prescription is found in the Word of God, where it clearly states that Jesus shed His blood for the remission of our sins. When the sin nature is taken care of in your life, you become empowered to experience the disciplined life as you daily crucify the flesh.

The Word of God shows us many ways to overcome the world to be a shining light; discipline is one of them. Winners are selective in what they eat. By sorting their food through careful examination of what is in their daily menu, they avoid the fats and the weights that constitute unnecessary burdens in life's journey. That was why Paul said in 1 Corinthians 9:27,

"But I discipline my body and bring *it* into subjection, lest, when I have preached to others, I myself should become disqualified."

With a daily life of self-examination, you can separate the chaff from the wheat. Sometimes, it's painstaking and laborious, but there can never be a testimony without a fight. The greater your fight, the greater testimony you will have.

There is one thing that cannot be argued about self-examination. It bestows a life of structure and discipline to anyone who daily walks in its path. Also, there is one thing you cannot argue about the big Mirror. You cannot hide anything from it. You can hide your sins from man, but you cannot hide them from yourself and from the eyes of the Word of God. If you love godliness and desire to be a jewel in the hands of God, make the Bible your friend. Though it's a mighty Mirror, it can fit into the hands of everyone. With it, you can dismantle the rusty wheels of any runaway habit of sin and gradually transform your unfruitful life into a life of fruitfulness; with it, you can transform your undisciplined life into a formidably disciplined life that people will emulate. To run from it is to run from peace, joy, and other blessings of God.

5. **It will show you how to walk daily in faith**

If you look into the Mirror of life daily, it will show you how to walk past the rudimentary things of life that your peers are still grappling with. It will show you how to **"Therefore, leaving the discussion of the elementary *principles* of Christ, let us go on to perfection, not laying again the foundation of repentance from dead works and of faith toward God, ..." (Hebrews 6:1).** With faith, you can accomplish what will take others a year or more to accomplish in a day. It has the power to open in an instant the door others have battled in vain for years to open.

You may be asking, how can I have this faith that can move mountains? The simple answer is to stay in the Word of God. Romans 10:17 says

"So then faith *comes* by hearing, and hearing by the word of God."

You can hear the Word of God through the gateway of the ear as it is being preached or taught by your pastor or through the silent voice of the Spirit of God as you read or study the Bible.

I grew up having a lot of fears. It got worse when I got into the University of Nigeria, Nsukka. I had feared I would die early; I had fears I would not have children; I had all kinds of terrible and numbing negative thoughts. One day I decided to do something about it. I left the campus and went to a church in the heart of Nsukka to see the pastor. I chose that church because I had a lot of respect for its founder. After narrating my ordeal to the pastor of the church, he gave me counsel that shocked me. He told me to go back to the campus and make the Bible my friend and that I would be alright. And because I was desperate, I adhered to his advice. It did the magic! As I devoured the Word of God daily, before I knew it, I was delivered from the belly of the abyss that constantly fed my heart with fears. Many do not know what they are doing to themselves by staying away from the daily study of the Word of God.

You may be going through hell right now and wondering

where God is. If you are patient soon, you will realize what is happening. Sometimes, God will take you through the tough terrains of life, but in the end, your rough edges will be smoothened. Before you fight a Goliath, He might first throw you into a boxing ring with a bear or a lion. But when you get into trouble, He will step into the ring and rescue you. This is how, sometimes, He builds your faith; or how you climb the ladder of faith. While you are going through that trial, make the Word of God your friend, and it will give you the needed strength to walk through that fire or treacherous water.

6. It will show you how to meditate

Meditation gives you the opportunity to discover God at a personal level. It makes God very real to you, more than the God your pastor or friends have told you about. It gives you the opportunity to behold Him in His holiness, majesty, power, love, and faithfulness. You cannot behold Him without being transformed. This accounts for why you have been in the church for over ten years, yet there is no real transformational change in your life and habits.

2 Corinthians 3:18 says,

"But we all, with unveiled face, beholding as in a mirror the glory of the Lord, are being transformed into the same image from glory to glory, just as [a]by the Spirit of the Lord."

When last did you hear from God? If you have children, you speak to them every time you are with them. Could it be why

God has not spoken to you lately, that you are hardly in His presence? Meditation transports you to the presence of God. It allows you to be still in the presence of God and allow Him to speak to you. It also gives you the opportunity to focus on the goodness, faithfulness, and mercies of God instead of focusing on your problems. Philippians 4:8 says,

"Finally, brethren, whatever things are true, whatever things *are* noble, whatever things *are* just, whatever things *are* pure, whatever things *are* lovely, whatever things *are* of good report, if *there is* any virtue and if *there is* anything praiseworthy—meditate on these things."

If you stay in the Word of God, you will stay out of dejection and defeat. If you remain in His Word, you will replace the darkness in your heart with light, the foul language in your mouth with words of gratitude and thanksgiving, and the lust in your eyes with holiness. As you meditate on His word, you will see what others don't see; you will hear what others are not capable of hearing, and you will experience the glory and presence of God others don't even know about. There is power and deliverance in meditating on the Word of God; there is a great blessing in standing before the Mirror and allowing God to show you secrets hidden from ordinary men. The world is wrapped in mystery, but the Mirror of God will unwrap it for you if you learn to stay in His Presence and wait for Him to speak.

7. **It will show you the Person of the Holy Spirit:**

An empty sack cannot stand upright until it's filled with something. You cannot be strong and stand upright for righteousness until you allow the Holy Spirit to fill you and to continue to refill you as you journey through life.

What you are filled with matters a lot. It determines your worth and your actions. If your heart is full of lust, you will fall for any craving you set your eyes on. If your heart is full of hatred, you will become a lethal weapon for racism and discrimination. If your heart is full of greed, you will steal from the poor to feed your greedy appetite. But when you are full of the Holy Spirit, you become a precious vessel, a mighty instrument in the hands of God.

Luke 6:45 says, **"A good man out of the good treasure of his heart brings forth good; and an evil man out of the evil treasure of his heart brings forth evil. For out of the abundance of the heart his mouth speaks."** Are you filled with the Word of God or with the antics of the world? Are you filled with the Word of God or with the aphorisms of the rich and the famous? A man who hears from God is a man who the Holy Spirit leads; a man who fills His life every day with the Word of God.

CHAPTER SIX

THE FOURTH LAW OF SELF-EXAMINATION

Let us search out and examine our ways,
And turn back to the Lord...
– Lamentations 3:40.

The fourth law of self-examination: ***If you don't soften the soil of your conscience with the pruning fork of self-examination, it will slowly harden.***

SOFTENING THE SOIL OF YOUR HEART

Before you can soften something, it must have come in a solid-state or must have hardened over time. And one thing that can harden over time is your heart. It could harden due to backsliding, spiritual ignorance, or blindness. Also, it could harden due to spiritual negligence, associations with the wrong crowd, or doctrine. The list is endless.

Ezekiel 36:26 says, **"I will give you a new heart and put a new spirit within you; I will take the heart of stone out of your flesh and give you a heart of flesh."**

It's always the will of our heavenly Father to give us what will help us become an instrument of blessing to Him, to our self, and to the world.

James 1:17 says, **"Every good gift and every perfect gift is from above, and comes down from the Father of lights, with whom there is no variation or shadow of turning."**

Apart from the physical blessings that include the air we breathe, the appetite for food, the sense of smell, touch, and hearing, to mention a few, there are also the spiritual blessings of God that begin with the gift of salvation. One of them is the exchange of hearts when you become born again: your stony heart is exchanged for the heart of flesh. Once God removes the stony, or the unbelieving, unlit, and selfish heart from you, and gives you a new heart, the responsibility shifts from Him to you to preserve what He has given you.

You have received too many things from God, some of which you are not even aware of. If Tiger Woods was not taken golfing at an early age by his father, he would not have discovered that he was very good at golf and that he could become the best golfer that ever lived on earth. If Venus and Serena Williams were not taken to the tennis courts to train at an early age by their father, they would not have discovered they could one day be two famous tennis players in the world.

Many others discovered their talents without the help of their parents or the help of others. While he was taking care of his father's sheep at the backside of the desert, the young biblical

David discovered he could play the violin and write poems and Psalms. Many of us go through life not discovering the gifts we have. Too many people that go around blaming God for their condition would be surprised the day they meet God to find out great gifts God gave them that were undiscovered, gifts that would have written the histories of their lives differently.

Work it out

The two greatest gifts are life and salvation. What are you doing with these two gifts? There are too many things bestowed upon you with salvation. Without self-examination, you may not be able to maximize them and use them to turn your life into greatness.

In Philippians 2:12-13, the Christian is given a very important advice:

"Therefore, my beloved, as you have always obeyed, not as in my presence only, but now much more in my absence, work out your own salvation with fear and trembling; for it is God who works in you both to will and to do for *His* good pleasure."

The above scriptural verses are strong proponents of the place of self-examination in a Christian's life. They are the summation of the Christian's part of the assignment and God's part. The summation here is that we have work to do; we have to work out our salvation, which includes working out a plan, working out a strategy, working out some steps needed to climb certain mountains, and working out some methodologies to overcome difficult people or peer pressures. There is work for you to do, for **"Thus also faith by itself, if it does not have works, is dead" (James 2:17).**

Even in the process of salvation, there is work involved. Romans 10:9 says, **"... if you confess with your mouth the Lord Jesus and believe in your heart that God has raised Him from the dead, you will be saved."**

For salvation to be complete, you have to open your mouth and declare that you are making Jesus the Lord of your life.

How do you daily work out your salvation?

Well, among other things, through a life of self-examination, a Christian can work to grow his Christian faith or walk. He can work to keep the light of his salvation from being extinguished; he can work from being a baby to being a mature Christian. Every day there are so many things working to put off your light, so to keep your light as bright as possible, you have to do a few more things along with self-examination. They include:

- **Prayer:** Pray every morning, at minimum for about thirty minutes. Some more mature Christians pray about three times a day for at least an hour each time. Anyone who says prayer does not work has not prayed before.
- **Bible Study:** Read and study your Bible every day. Combine the use of the printed copy of the Bible and electronic versions. For spiritual strength, you must devour the Bible voraciously and methodically. 2

Timothy 2:15 demands that you **"Be diligent to present yourself approved to God, a worker who does not need to be ashamed, rightly dividing the word of truth."**

Every Christian is called to study the Bible so well that it gets the approval of God. No one is exempted from the great assignment of being well equipped with the Bible and properly defending the truth it bears. How equipped are you? Can you really defend the Gospel through your life and the knowledge of the Word of God in you?

- **Fellowship:** Fellowshipping with brethren requires time, money, and physical energy. Fellowship provides a worship time and a relationship with God and other brethren in the church or a house fellowship or other Christian associations.
- **Service:** Through service, you become the hands and feet of Jesus Christ, His mouthpiece, His foot soldier, etc. Through service, you become God's battle-axe, His ambassador, etc. Through service, you become an extension of God's kingdom, spreading the light and Gospel of the kingdom.

Service is our number one call. Every believer is called to **"Go into all the world and preach the gospel to every creature. He who believes and is baptized will be saved; but he who does not believe will be condemned" (Mark 16:15-16).** The emphasis of the above scripture is "going to the world." I believe the Christian's greatest assignment is outside the four walls of the church.

The church is a fuel station where you go to fuel up spiritually. It is not a place to spend all your time in like most Christians do today. They go to church four to five times a week and end up having no time for their families, no time to discover their gifts, no time to build up their personal prayer life and Bible study. This type of lifestyle leaves no time for the Christian to preach the Gospel to the dying world.

I believe in balanced Christianity. A lot of Christians are on their pastor's leash. He drags them in any direction he wishes! Unfortunately, such people have been so brainwashed that they can't see and hear the truth beyond what their pastors tell them. Your local church should not so preoccupy you that you have no time for other things that are of eternal value. There is more work to do in your closet, building up yourself spiritually, plus work to do outside the church, reaching the unsaved who are being dragged to hell every day by Satan. You have to have a spiritually balanced life; otherwise, you will tilt badly in the wrong direction with great repercussions.

- **Giving:** Giving is a type of service. It's a service that seems to have quick results and a far-reaching effect than we can ever imagine. There is nothing greater than bringing smiles to people's faces through meeting their needs or giving hope to someone by turning their life around through giving. If you don't know that giving is hard work, you have not really given anything of value.

Work your promises

All of the promises of God, with no exception, have a condition attached to them. There is a requirement you have to meet before any promise becomes a reality in your life. So, when you engage in working out your salvation, you are not violating grace, or faith, or the unction or function of the Holy Spirit. No, what you are simply doing is playing your own part in the deal with God; or keeping your own part of the bargain with God.

Folding your hands and waiting for manna to fall from heaven is an abdication of your divine assignment, and that explains why many Christians today do not have tangible results befitting of blood-washed, faith-filled, blessed, and ordained children of God. When you fold your hands from day to day and refuse to work the work, you will walk around, a poor and wretched Christian. The word of God works for those who work it until it works. If you put no seed in the ground, you have no right to expect any harvest.

A mature Christian is that Christian who knows what his responsibility is and daily labors for it through the grace and enablement of Christ. You must do the hard work; you must go through the process of laboring, even when there is a possibility of failure. Some works require special armors (Ephesians 6:10-18), some require fasting (Matthew 17:21), some require violent disposition (Matthew 11:12), and some require wisdom and revelation from the Holy Spirit while some require rugged faith. But, fight we must, work we must, because no serious Christian is counted among those who sleep while others are at war.

"But we are not of those who draw back to perdition, but of those who believe to the saving of the soul" (Hebrews 10:39).

Simply put, it is hard to work out your salvation without a consistent life of self-examination. It's hard to soften the soil of your heart without living a life of regular self-examination. Self-examination is the hoe to weed your path so you can run and not stumble. It is the big reminder board to remind you to keep your eyes on the target to help you reach your destination. It is the light that, when you keep it shining on your conscience, will keep it always awake and sensitive to the Holy Spirit. You can accomplish much in life with a life that has a living conscience.

YOUR CONSCIENCE: DEAD OR ALIVE?

The conscience comes into play in every decision you make. It's the inner voice that talks to you every day. Sadly, a lot of people have closed the door of their conscience. They have shuttered it with the bolts of self-delusion and pride. They have bolted its door with the rod of greed and the mundane things of the world. Some people have buried their conscience in the putrid tomb of pleasures and self-glory. And by so doing, they have turned off the internal warning signs planted in every mortal by God, exposing themselves to untold dangers every day they walk on the surface of the earth.

When you live with a dead conscience, you are simply living to do the biddings of the devil. This is why the devil is turning off the light in people's consciences every minute of the day and blindfolding them. They can't tell the difference between good and bad, light and darkness, or white and black with the blindfolds.

No one is wiser than God. God gave a man a conscience because He knew at creation that man would need it. He knew at creation it would be dangerous for man to walk the earth where the devil is roaming around, without an inbuilt warning system. It's the conscience that sounds the alarm when your ship is sinking so that you can find a way of escape. It's the conscience that receives the warning message from the radar when your flight is heading in the wrong direction and flashes it on the dashboard of your heart to help you avert flying into a mountain. When you live with a sick conscience, you endanger your life, family, and the society.

What is the state of your conscience? Do you really care whose toe you step on to achieve your dreams? Do you care who you push off the road to get to your destination? Paul's testimony to the Sanhedrin is,

"Men *and* brethren, I have lived in all good conscience before God until this day" (Acts 23:1).

What is your testimony in your workplace, your church, or in your family? The last time you were offended, what testimony did you leave behind? The last time you were put in charge of a department, what testimony did you leave behind? Your conscience plays a significant part in the footprints you leave behind each day.

TYPES OF CONSCIENCE

There are three types of conscience I know. Let's take a closer look at each of them.

1. DYING CONSCIENCE

The parable of the Good Samaritan is an important parable. It has a lot to teach us about the conscience of man.

Then Jesus answered and said: "A certain *man* went down from Jerusalem to Jericho, and fell among thieves, who stripped him of his clothing, wounded *him,* and departed, leaving *him* half dead. Now by chance a certain priest came down that road. And when he saw him, he passed by on the other side. Likewise, a Levite, when he arrived at the place, came and looked, and passed by on the other side. But a certain Samaritan, as he journeyed, came where he was. And when he saw him, he had compassion. So he went to *him* and bandaged his wounds, pouring on oil and wine; and he set him on his own animal, brought him to an inn, and took care of him. On the next day, when he departed, he took out two denarii, gave *them* to the innkeeper, and said to him, 'Take care of him; and whatever more you spend, when I come again, I will repay

you.' So which of these three do you think was neighbor to him who fell among the thieves?"

And he said, "He who showed mercy on him."

Then Jesus said to him, "Go and do likewise."

- Luke 10:30-37.

A closer look at this story reveals that action speaks louder than words. It's not the size of your Bible that matters; it's not the number of titles you append to your name that matters; it's not your chieftaincy title or your gold-trimmed priestly robe that matters. What matters most are your everyday actions.

The Bible says you will be known by the fruits you bear (Matthew 7:16). The priest and the descendant of Levi who saw a man who was bathed in his own blood and felt they had something else more important to attend to than saving the dying man's life certainly have a problem with their conscience. They have a sick or a dying conscience.

When a conscience is dying, it gravitates to doing only convenient things; things that people will applaud; things that please the flesh and stroke the ego. A dying conscience makes little or no sacrifice for others. A dying conscience is one of the marks of a backsliding Christian or those who prefer to mitigate the smell of their putrefying lifestyles with the sweet aroma of their colognes. The sad thing is that their lives will smell good only for few hours before their rotten smell returns.

The Present-day Clergy

Since the Good Samaritan story highlights the unbecoming behaviors of two ancient clergymen, let's take a closer look at the unbecoming behaviors of the present-day clergy. There abound many African pastors who started their ministry with humble and meek hearts, but as their churches grew, they slowly became obsessed with money, power, and fame until they took up personalities that are far removed from the Person of Christ. In some of their branch churches, you will hear more of the praises of "Daddies" (these pastors) than the praises of God, the heavenly Daddy. These are pastors who were once humble, now sharing the glory of God in their bid to bring every member to their lordship and control. I have always asked myself where the conscience of every one of these pastors who relish in human worship and treat the children of God as cows muzzled and huddled into a room for tutelage on how to bow to them?

Too many of us have forgotten the reason Lucifer was cast down from heaven. He tried to rub shoulders with God, which is a very dangerous thing to do. Some of these pastors, knowingly or unknowingly, are stealing the glory of God. Lucifer tried it and was crushed.

> **"How you are fallen from heaven,**
> **O Lucifer, son of the morning!**
> ***How* you are cut down to the ground,**
> **You who weakened the nations!**
> **For you have said in your heart:**

'I will ascend into heaven,
I will exalt my throne above the stars of God;
I will also sit on the mount of the congregation
On the farthest sides of the north;
I will ascend above the heights of the clouds,
I will be like the Most High.'
Yet you shall be brought down to Sheol,
To the lowest depths of the Pit.

- Isaiah 14:12-15

Oh, what a fall for Lucifer, from glory to the lowest depths of the pit! How I pity pastors trading places with God. In their lust for power, they twist their messages; in their bid to be the only voice that is heard, they set up ungodly decrees; in their bid to control the church money and use it anyway they want, they strip power from everyone but themselves and their family members.

Jeremiah 23:25-26 says, **"I have heard what the prophets have said who prophesy lies in My name, saying, 'I have dreamed, I have dreamed!' How long will *this* be in the heart of the prophets who prophesy lies? Indeed, *they are* prophets of the deceit of their own heart, ..."**

This is why I warn people to be careful whose message they consume. Do not subscribe wholly to the teachings of any pastor who has not submitted himself totally to God. And do not attend a church that is not totally surrendered to God; otherwise, you will be robbed and wounded and fed a diet of lies that will not take you close to the gate of heaven.

You have to respect and honor your pastor and all those in authority, and you have to do it with the right motive. But please don't swallow everything from the pulpit; a lot of them are from the flesh. Be like the Berean Christians. Here is what Acts 17:11 says about them:

"These were more [d]fair-minded than those in Thessalonica, in that they received the word with all readiness, and searched the Scriptures daily *to find out* whether these things were so."

Remember, we are in the last days: days when the truth will be scarce; days when many people are not what they say they are. These are days we have to re-evaluate our lives every day through the clear lens of the Bible. If you don't, before you knew it, you will be walking around with a dying or dead conscience even with a big Bible in your hands.

2. DEAD CONSCIENCE

A dead conscience is a conscience that is so hardened that it does not respond to the stimulus of the Holy Spirit. It has no place for remorse or guilt. When a person's conscience is as callous as a rock, he will be selfish to the point that he does not care about the life or death of others. He can go to any length to have whatever he wants, be it money or position. Such a person walks around with a conscience that has been seared with a hot iron, a conscience that suppresses the truth, and has completely closed its door to Truth and the Author of Truth (Romans 1:18).

It's commonplace to find African politicians whose consciences are dead. While millions of Africans are dying in poverty every week, they are busy looting every penny from the government coffers. And when the coffers run dry, they turn around and borrow billions of dollars from all over the world to continue to feed their greed.

Africa is a continent under siege. Every day it's being plundered by indigenous politicians and their foreign collaborators. It's being exploited by those with dead consciences that don't give a hoot about the millions of African children dying every year from malnutrition. When the conscience of man is dead, he does not care if the rest of the country dies as long as he is basking in opulence with the money looted from his country's coffers.

A dead conscience is not only peculiar to politicians. It's a place anybody who does not examine his or her life daily can slip into. It does not matter who you are; the day you stop responding to the voice of the Holy Spirit is the day your conscience starts dying. The longer you resist the Spirit of God, the more your conscience dies until it's completely dead. But if you soften the soil of your conscience with the pruning fork of self-examination and the Sword of the Spirit, which is the word of God, it will not ever harden.

3. THE LIVING CONSCIENCE

A living conscience is a conscience that is sensitive to the leading of God. It quickly responds to the promptings of the Holy Spirit. It is sensitive to the needs of others and the demands of God. It was the type of conscience Paul testified of in 2 Corinthians 1:12. It says,

" For our boasting is this: the testimony of our conscience that we conducted ourselves in the world in simplicity and godly sincerity, not with fleshly wisdom but by the grace of God, and more abundantly toward you."

What do your actions testify about you? What does your word testify about you? No Christian without a living conscience is worth emulating.

Living conscience was the type of conscience Daniel had when he refused to defile himself with the king's meat in Daniel 1:8. It says, **"But Daniel purposed in his heart that he would not defile himself with the portion of the king's delicacies, nor with the wine which he drank; therefore, he requested of the chief of the eunuchs that he might not defile himself."**

It was the type of conscience Joseph had when he rejected the sexual overtures of his master's wife. The Bible states, **"But he refused and said to his master's wife, "Look, my master does not know what *is* with me in the house, and he has committed all that he has to my hand. *There is* no one greater in this house than I, nor has he kept back anything from me but you, because you *are* his wife. How then can I do this great wickedness, and sin against God?" (Genesis 39:8-9).**

It was the type of conscience Moses had when he chose to suffer with his people. The book of Hebrews says, **"By faith Moses,**

when he became of age, refused to be called the son of Pharaoh's daughter, choosing rather to suffer affliction with the people of God than to enjoy the passing pleasures of sin, esteeming the reproach of Christ greater riches than the treasures in Egypt; for he looked to the reward" (Hebrews 11:24-26).

It was the type of conscience Ruth had when she refused to leave Naomi. Ruth 1:16 says, " **Entreat me not to leave you,**
Or to **turn back from following after you;**
For wherever you go, I will go;
And wherever you lodge, I will lodge;
Your people ***shall be*** **my people,**
And your God, my God."

A living conscience is priceless. It sets preachers apart. It sets presidents apart. It was what distinguished the state of the heart of the Good Samaritan from the two clergymen. It will also distinguish you. But if you close the door of your heart to the daily life of self-examination, your conscience may harden. The good news is that no matter the state of your conscience today, God can recreate it if you allow Him. All you have to do is open the door of your heart and let Him take absolute control of it. There is no life God cannot use if surrendered to Him.

CHAPTER SEVEN

THE FIFTH LAW OF SELF-EXAMINATION

But let each one examine his own work, and then
he will have rejoicing in himself alone and not in another.
-Galatians 6:4

The fifth law of self-examination: ***The unexamined lifestyle is not worth living.***

A package left in the corner of a prominent building would be treated as a dangerous and suspicious item in today's world. It would be foolish for you to run down to its location, grab it and take it home, disregarding the possibility of it being a bomb that could detonate and blow you into shreds.

Unfortunately, that's precisely what most people do with their lives. They expose themselves to danger by living unexamined lives. They expose themselves to STDs and AIDS by living a sexually promiscuous lifestyle; they expose themselves to bullets and imprisonment by electing to join gangs. No matter how physically or spiritually strong you are, no unexamined path is worth treading. In the words of Socrates, "An unexamined life is not worth living."

THE EXAMINED LIFE

One of the ironies of life is that, sometimes, sweet things are hidden inside hard shells. In my family, we sometimes "fight" over coconut water. Each time my wife gives me a coconut to crack its shell, she waits anxiously with her big cup for a greater share of the sweet coconut water. In life, if you are not ready to crack the hard shells of precious virtues like self-examination, you will not enjoy their sweet harvests. The sweet taste of coconut water is enough incentive to do the hard work of breaking its shell. In the light of this truth, it should not be a surprise to you that the lifestyle of self-examination or the examined life does not come cheap. It can be a very hard shell to crack or a high price to pay.

A certain rich young man came to Jesus and inquired, **"What do I still lack?"** (Matthew 19:20). In the next verse, Jesus answered him, **"If you want to be perfect, go, sell what you have and give to the poor, and you will have treasure in heaven; and come, follow Me."** The response Jesus gave him was very profound. Jesus expounded in a nutshell what is missing in some churches today. If there is anything in your life that you can't give up for Jesus, you cannot faithfully serve Him. If you want to follow Christ, you must not put anything between you and Him; not your money, title, or church; not your pastor, job, or anything whatsoever.

Christianity today has been reduced to church worship, pastor worship, status worship, money worship, and the worship of so many things that drive a wedge between Jesus and us. In the above scripture, Jesus was simply saying to the rich man to forfeit the most precious possession he has before he qualifies to follow Him. It's easy for us to be possessed by our possessions. Anything that possesses you becomes your master, and once you have another master, Jesus cannot be your master also. You cannot serve two masters.

Matthew 6:24 clearly states, **"No one can serve two masters; for either he will hate the one and love the other, or else he will be loyal to the one and despise the other. You cannot serve God and mammon."**

The unfortunate thing is that many people think they are serving God, not knowing they are serving tables. They go to church, but like the rich man, they are unwilling to give up their wealth or the lifestyle they derive pleasure from. They go to church but are unwilling to give up their boyfriends or girlfriends; they go to church but are unwilling to give up going to nightclubs and alcohol joints or bars.

Jesus knew the rich man's wealth was his god, and that's why He demanded he gives it up before he can follow Him. To you, Jesus probably would have told you to sell your car, if that is an idol to you; or to go and tender your resignation for your job, if it is a god to you; or Jesus could have told you to stop worshipping your thrones, crowns, titles, men, fame, or money before you can follow him.

Some are poor today because they refused to pay the price of acquiring a college or university degree. Most people live below their worth. They lack the courage to fight and the patience to keep on fighting. They rob themselves of the opportunity to make their lives count. Also, they rob their children of the opportunity to climb on their shoulders to greater heights.

Myles Munroe once said, **"The wealthiest place on the planet is just down the road. It is the cemetery. There lie buried companies that were never started, inventions that were never made, bestselling books that were never written, and masterpieces that were never painted. In the cemetery is buried the greatest treasure of untapped potential."**

This is a sad truth. And the reason behind it is that too many people don't want to pay the price for greatness. They want gold but don't want to go through the refining fire; they want to be another King David but don't want to kill a Goliath; they want to be another Daniel but don't want to be thrown into a lion's den; they want to have the success story of the three Hebrew men but don't want to be thrown into a lake of fire.

Every redeemed child of God has a wonderful heritage. The question is, how do you manifest this glory? Every redeemed child of God has been given great authority, but how do you walk in this great authority? Every redeemed child of God has been given enormous possessions, but how do you possess these possessions? The Bible is replete with the story of ordinary men and women who accomplished great things for mankind and for the kingdom of God through faith and patience; so, you have no excuse (Hebrews 11).

Every day gives you another opportunity to walk the narrow

road of self-examination and to chart your course towards freedom. Every day gives you the opportunity to examine your ways (Haggai 1:5,7). We are on a daily journey called life, and one day we will get to the finish line.

When the end comes, will you like Paul, boldly testify, **"I have fought a good fight, I have finished the race, I have kept the faith"** (2 Timothy 4:7)? When at the end of your journey you meet your Maker, will He say to you, **"'Well *done,* good and faithful servant; you were faithful over a few things, I will make you ruler over many things. Enter into the joy of your lord" (Matthew 25:21).**

If you want to have the testimony of Paul, you have to pay the price of taking the Gospel of our Lord Jesus Christ to the Gentiles; pay the price of being arrested and imprisoned for the Gospel; traveling through Asia, Greece, and many dangerous places, and planting churches he never later monopolized. If you want to stop the mouth of lions like Daniel, you have to pay the price of an endless prayer life. If you want to wear the heavenly crown of gold, you have to first wear the earthly crown of thorns. There is a price to pay to live a purposeful and an examined life.

AREAS TO CONSTANTLY EXAMINE

There are areas of your life you should examine every day if you are earnestly contending for the faith, preparing, and waiting for the return of the Lord. There are areas of your life that demand daily attention if you want to be a light and a salt (Matthew 5:13-16); a true ambassador of Jesus Christ at a time when the cross of Christ has become heavier and the road to heaven narrower (2 Corinthian 5:20).

Kings don't commonize themselves. They carry a certain air of dignity and would not condescend to certain unbecoming behaviors. The same is true for any Christian who knows he or she is special. You should know that "... **you *are* a chosen generation, a royal priesthood, a holy nation, His own special people, that you may proclaim the praises of Him who called you out of darkness into His marvelous light; who once *were* not a people but *are* now the people of God, who had not obtained mercy but now have obtained mercy" (1 Peter 2:9-10)**.

And if indeed you believe this scripture, you cannot afford to live an unexamined life.

1. **Examine the paths you are traveling**

Many early explorers died in their journeys by sea and land because they had no knowledge of what lay ahead or the existing dangers that awaited them. Some knew the risks and still ventured into unchartered territories; many of them perished in the dark abysmal belly of high seas and were shortly forgotten.

The destinies of many people have been ruined; the lives of many great minds and gifted souls have been cut short because they plunged into an unexamined lifestyle. Remember the old saying, "all that glitters is not gold." Take time and do your research before you accept an invitation to try something new.

A neighbor may say to you, "Oh, come to our church; we love everybody!" That sounds great! However, find out first if he or she loves Jesus before you visit the church.

Someone else might invite you to a party or an adventure that seemingly looks harmless. Get the facts before you accept such an invitation. It might be a cult or a party where drugs and illicit sex are peddled. Take time to investigate any pathway of life before you travel through it. It might cost you the denial of little fun; it might rob you the temporary joy of feasting your eyes; or the cost might be depriving yourself of certain questionable riches, but in the end, you will save yourself a lot of tears and pains. Remember what Matthew 24:12-13 says,

"And because lawlessness will abound, the love of many will grow cold. But he who endures to the end shall be saved."

2. **Examine the words you speak**

Words can be a piercing sword or a soothing balm. Words can be destructive or constructive. Unexamined words come out carelessly, thoughtlessly, and recklessly. They have the potential to kill or cause serious harm. But kind words coming out of a kind heart have the potential to calm the storm in someone's life. Be mindful of the words you speak. Once they come out of your mouth, you cannot retract them. Proverbs 15:1 says, **"A soft answer turns away wrath, But a harsh word stirs up anger."**

Not only can you destroy others, but you can also destroy

yourself with the words you speak. I recall overhearing someone telling a co-worker he might not live to see the 2000 Atlanta summer Olympics, and sure enough, before the Olympics began, he died. He did not look sick to me when he spoke those negative words over his life. Words are powerful. Negative words are like arrows; they kill!

Proverb 18:21 says,

"Death and life *are* in the power of the tongue, And those who love it will eat its fruit."

The unexamined word is not worth uttering.

3. **Examine the friends you keep.**

If you stick around a contaminated environment for too long, your lungs may become compromised by the contaminant. A bad friend is like an infectious disease. They carry deadly pathogens that can easily infect you if you regularly hang out with them. If you keep going out with a drug dealer, soon you may become one or learn how to use drugs. The stories abound of some teenagers who were deceived by drug peddlers' flashy lifestyle and made the mistake of abandoning their education and towing the footsteps of these bad apples. They ended up in prison.

On the contrary, good friends are like good medicine. They soothe your pains and heal your wounds. They bring out the best in you by helping to put out any fire that wants to engulf you. They tell you the truth even when it hurts, but they do it with love. A friend with a questionable lifestyle is not worth having.

Some people may come to you and pretend to be your friends, but they are wolves in sheep's clothing. I had a recent experience that shook me to the bones. It forced me to accept the truth that some people you consider your friends can be extremely evil and go to any length to destroy you, regardless of their religious titles. Sometimes, all it takes for you to suddenly become an enemy is a little promotion in your workplace, or a house better than theirs, or a car better than theirs. After that bad experience, I have learned to choose my friends very carefully. People are not what they seem. Choose your friends carefully and prayerfully, and you will save yourself a lot of pain and anguish.

Proverbs 18:24 says,

"A man *who has* friends must himself be friendly, But there is a friend *who* sticks closer than a brother."

4. **Examine the books you read.**

Books are great assets, but they can also be poisonous. A bad book can cast a fog over your mind, and before you know it, you have consumed enough of it to poison your soul. A lot of poisons are hidden in books, and many lives have been ruined because they fell into the traps of mysticism, cultism, atheism, racism, or downright religious bigotry; all hidden in finely printed and great-looking books.

The books you are attracted to speak much about the state of your heart or things that fascinate you. I recall a younger lady

I knew in my teenage days. She introduced me to romance novels. She was obsessed with every romantic author and their books. Eventually, she started copying some of the books' romantic escapades, which almost ruined her life.

Galatians 5:9 says, **"A little leaven leavens the whole lump."** Be careful with what books you read. The greatest book in the world is the Bible. Make it your friend, and your life will never remain the same.

5. **Examine what you watch**

Be careful what you watch on your phone, laptop, and TV. If this is the only useful thing I wrote in this book, then I have not wasted my time. No time in history is this truer than today. Every time you turn on the TV, you are inundated with filth and things that can defile the soul. Every time you browse the internet, you are bombarded with filthy things that can desecrate the soul. The same is true about cell phones.

We live in a time that calls for caution if you really want to make heaven. Thoroughly examine what you watch on your cell phone, computer, and TV; otherwise, you may end up being ensnared and sucked into things like pornography. As important as they are, these three gadgets have been responsible for sowing seeds of immorality in the lives of people more than anything else in the history of mankind.

The eye is a very important gateway to the soul of man, and if you want to remain spiritually fit for the work of the kingdom of God, you have to be very careful of what you feed your eyes.

The Bible says,

"The lamp of the body is the eye. If therefore your eye is good, your whole body will be full of light. But if your eye is bad, your whole body will be full of darkness. If therefore the light that is in you is darkness, how great *is* that darkness!" (Matthew 6:22-23).

6. **Examine what you hear**

The ear is another essential gateway to the soul of man. It feeds the mind with information. If you continue to stuff garbage into your ears, with time, it will poison your mind, and eventually, your whole being. But if you feed the ear with the enriching words, you will plant great seeds of faith and wisdom in your heart which will eventually propel you through difficult times of life.

Judge what you hear, be it music or a Christian message or advice. John 5:30 says,

"I can of Myself do nothing. As I hear, I judge; and My judgment is righteous, because I do not seek My own will but the will of the Father who sent Me."

Do you judge what you hear like our Master Jesus, or do you allow your ears to be a garbage bin? Music is powerful; it has a way of grabbing someone's attention, and if you are not careful, it can hold your mind captive for a while. When I got born-again in the seventies, I was taught to **"Abstain from every form of evil" (1 Thessalonians 5:22).** What happened to those good old messages? I don't hear them anymore from the pulpits. Abstain from worldly music; they are not good for your soul. They will pollute your spirit and open you to the seductive spirit of the world.

Anything that cannot feed your faith is not worth feeding your ears. Any word or advice that does not edify is not worth consuming. Anything that does not add value to your life is not worth the attention of your ears. Guard your ears. They are very important gateways. Mark 4:24 says, "Then He said to them, **"Take heed what you hear. With the same measure you use, it will be measured to you; and to you who hear, more will be given."**

7. **Examine the food you eat.**

Many do not realize that the greatest medicine given to us by God is food. Before you put any food in your mouth, be sure it's the medicine your body needs. Bad foods are toxic to the body. Avoid them, and you will save yourself a lot of trouble and heartaches.

There are Christians who have made fasting a lifestyle. They are great arsenals in the hands of God. Great men and women of God are those who die daily on their knees and through fasting. When they rise from their knees, they stand tall above others. They make their food the word of God, knowing that **"It is written, 'Man shall not live by bread alone, but by every word that proceeds from the mouth of God" (Matthew 4:4).**

8. **Examine the clothes you wear**

What you wear speaks volumes about your character, your taste, your values, and your personality. When a woman wears revealing clothes, she cheapens herself. You are not different from what you wear. It reveals the face behind the mask; it reveals your true image. I question the salvation experience that does not translate into what a person wears.

I promised a pastor I met many times in a prayer meeting that I was going to visit his church. So, one day I did, because I had to keep my word. For whatever reason, at a point during the church service, he said on the pulpit that he does not give the microphone to any type of person, a statement I have heard many pastors make. Unfortunately, most choir members who sang on the platform with the church microphones wore very tight revealing pants and other unholy attires that troubled me so much in my spirit. After a while, it became obvious to me where they copied that type of dressing. It was from the pastor's wife, who had a skirt that hugged her buttocks so hard that it was disgusting to see. If our dressing is the same as the dressing of the world, then what is the difference between light and darkness, the church and the world, or the believer and the unbeliever?

There are those who are decent enough to keep their party clothes out of the church, but that does not make it any better. A Christian is not supposed to have two lifestyles or wear two faces, one for the church and one for life outside the church. That is the lifestyle of the Pharisees. We can't serve God and Mammon. Who is your God, the god of fashion or the God of heaven? When will you start living for God and not for every fashion and fad that crosses your eyes, whether it is edifying or not? Joshua 24:15 says,

"And if it seems evil to you to serve the LORD, choose for yourselves this day whom you will serve, whether the gods which your fathers served that *were* on the other side of the River, or the gods of the Amorites, in whose land you dwell. But as for me and my house, we will serve the LORD."

Many people are working for the devil without knowing it. When you parade yourself in an ungodly attire, you are walking on Satan's runway, displaying his outfit to others shopping for the wares of the devil. When you are in an unholy alliance with the opposite sex, you are helping the devil build his network and expand his kingdom. Always ask yourself, "Is what I am doing benefitting the kingdom of God, or is it benefitting the kingdom of darkness?" Make this question the acid test for your dressing.

9. **Examine the church you go to.**

Many years ago, I traveled to Calabar, a city in Nigeria. I had my own business, and I was there to sell my products. After checking into a hotel, I decided to visit a church; I saw its sign while driving down to the hotel. When I got to the church premises, I found out that it was not a real church; it was a cult building. The owner of the supposed church prays for anyone who visits his building. So, when he elected to pray for me, I declined. Then he said something that shocked me. He said, "You are the only person who has stepped on this ground that has refused my prayers." As quickly as I could, I dashed out of the premises and headed back to my hotel.

My point is that it's not everything that looks like a church that is truly a church. Some churches today are merely private businesses families are running to make a living. Some are merely social clubs where people come to wheel and deal and to make new friends. Any church not totally surrendered to the Lordship of Jesus Christ is not worth your time and money. Any church shrouded in secrecy or lacking transparency is not worth your time. These are the last days. Watch your footsteps; watch the pews and the pulpits. Don't be careless with your soul.

10. Examine your daily life

Examine the life you are living because people are watching you. The type of life you are living will determine the type of people you will attract. A woman who keeps attracting the wrong suitor is living an unexamined life. The same is true for men. What kind of people do you attract? We can't hide who we are for too long. If you have no moral boundaries, soon people will know, and those who love that type of lifestyle will gravitate to you.

Years ago, on the college campus, someone I wasn't too close to stopped me and thanked me for the kind of life I was living. I was thrown aback by his kind words because although we were both in the same faculty, we were not close. I was shocked to know that he had been watching me over the years. To be honest, I didn't know my lifestyle was influencing or affecting him. I was still a young Christian whose light was probably dim, yet the light was bright enough for him to see.

The life we live can lighten or darken the paths of others. It can attract angels, or it can attract demons. It can attract the right people or the wrong people to you. Examine your life today. Examine the fruit you are bearing.

Examine the footprints you are leaving behind. One day your life will come to an end. How will you be remembered? What kind of footprints will you leave? Will you like Paul say **"I have fought the good fight, I have finished the race, I have kept the faith. Finally, there is laid up for me the crown of righteousness, which the Lord, the righteous Judge, will give to me on that Day, and not to me only but also to all who have loved His appearing"** (2 Timothy 4:7-8).

Life is short. It's therefore not wise to continue to put off living a daily life of self-examination. Begin today and watch the great values it will add to your life. Every day, make it a habit to **"Examine yourselves *as to* whether you are in the faith. Test yourselves. Do you not know yourselves, that Jesus Christ is in you? —unless indeed you are disqualified"** (2 Corinthians 13:5).

CHAPTER EIGHT

THE SIXTH LAW OF SELF-EXAMINATION

"You have sown much, and bring in little; You eat, but do not have enough; You drink, but you are not filled with drink; You clothe yourselves, but no one is warm;
And he who earns wages, earns wages to put into a bag with holes." – Haggai 1:5-7

The sixth law of self-examination: ***Self-examination without divinity is futility.***

It's crucial at this point to emphasize that self-examination without divine enablement may amount to futility. You may never have total freedom until you enlist the help of the Author of Freedom. When you partner with God, the One who is all-knowing, all-powerful, the Creator of mankind and the universe, the One who has never lost a battle, you will be unbeatable.

There are battles in your life you can never win with human strength. As wonderful and useful as self-examination is, some battles go beyond it; and like every other human effort, it has its own limits, but it makes a wonderful pair with the supreme power of God.

The greatest miracles are not calling down fire from heaven, walking on water, or having a child after twenty years of barrenness. The greatest miracle on earth is the miracle of the new birth that happens when someone accepts Jesus Christ as his Lord and Savior. How many times have you made New Year resolutions and never kept them? How many times have you decided to break a bad habit and failed? The reason is that there are specific battles the flesh and self-will cannot win for you. There are fights that you cannot win without the help of God; that's why you need to surrender your life to Him in order to give Him the legal authority to fight your battles for you.

Jeremiah 17:5 says,

Thus says the LORD:
"Cursed *is* the man who trusts in man
And makes flesh his strength,
Whose heart departs from the LORD."

A wise man does not fight spiritual battles with the flesh because he knows the flesh is not a match for principalities and powers of darkness that operate in high places. Philippians 3:3 puts it this way, **"For we are the circumcision, who worship God in the Spirit, rejoice in Christ Jesus, and have no confidence in the flesh,..."**

Ephesians 6:12 expounds this truth even further. It says, **"For we do not wrestle against flesh and blood, but against principalities, against powers, against the rulers of the darkness of this age, against spiritual *hosts* of wickedness in the heavenly *places*."**

There are certain things in life you cannot do for yourself; try as you may. No psychologist or motivational speaker can equip you with enough skill to blot away your transgressions. No professor can impart to you the power to break the stronghold of sin in your life. It will take the cleansing blood of Jesus to purge you of your sins. Until you cry out to Him to save you and until you run to Him with your sins and lay them at his feet, you will remain defeated, no matter how many times you make or renew your new-year resolutions; or how many self-help books you read.

To have better results in the exercise of self-examination, you need to begin at the cross. It's at the cross the exchange for your sins was made through the crucifixion of Jesus Christ. There you can exchange your weakness for strength; your sickness for divine health; there, your battles will be taken over by our Savior and Redeemer. Your personal efforts will fail you in certain journeys of life. No man is a match for the devil whose goal is to steal, kill, and destroy your purpose and your life (John 10:10).

The spiritually blind cannot see beyond his desires, wants, feelings, thirst, and hunger for the praise and accolades of others. But when the Holy Spirit takes over your life, He reveals all things to you, the hidden things and the unhidden things you still can't see. John 16:13 says, **"However, when He, the Spirit of truth, has come, He will guide you into all truth; for He will not speak on His own *authority,* but whatever He hears, He will speak; and He will tell you things to come."**

There is no salvation in that lofty career or job you relish so much; there is no salvation in any citadel of learning; there is no salvation in being the citizen of any nation or through your family name. Acts 4:12 says, **"Nor is there salvation in any other, for there is no other name under heaven given among men by which we must be saved."** Jesus is the only Savior of mankind!

Take everything to the Lord. Take your battles, pains, and dreams, and exchange them for His grace, mercy, unfailing compassion, and love. I did that about forty-five years ago, and I am so glad I did. I summarized my salvation experience in one of my poems titled; ***I Found a Friend.***

I FOUND A FRIEND

When you abdicated your throne in heaven
and came looking for me,
I knew I had found a friend.

You did not come showing your crown
or the smacks of the cross;
you did not come with lamentation or condemnation.
You came calling my name

with the voice of compassion,
you came reaching for me
with your healing and atoning blood!

You saw me in ashes, in smoke,
in rubble, in frosty grime;
you saw me in captive chains,
in the dark dingy pit of sin
and you rescued me.

Like a flute echoing in the wood,
like the serenade of moonlight,
like the circus of a million stars,
your love swiftly seized my heart.

When You touched my leprous skin
my mask and marks of shame melted
in the flame of your grace and glory
and my face came blazing
with the joy of a new life.

I had nothing to give to you;
nothing to give my Savior,
nothing but what was left of me:
mind dulled by the blunt edges of darkness,
hands and legs ribbed
by the rusty chains of slavery,
eyes eroded by tears
and bitter waters of sorrow.

Yet you took me,
you took what was left of me,

you took my tatters and my shreds
and made something out of me.

Yes, God can make something out of you; out of what is left of your journey, out of what is left of your battered life if you give him a chance. He specializes in mending broken hearts. He has a balm that can heal any wound. He is the Potter; He specializes in piecing together the broken clays of our lives and giving us a new image. No life can break to the point that God cannot mend. He is the Master of impossibilities.

He did not promise that all will be easy. For me, the forty-five years journey of following Christ has not been easy. Every day brings the sound of a new battle; every day brings the drumbeat of a new roaring storm. One would have thought that after all these years of climbing many dubious hills of life and wrestling with different treacherous shifting sands and sand dunes and weathering endless harsh winters and angry seas of life, that the journey would have been a lot easier. If the truth be told, I still stub my toes; I still stop to sit and whine; one would have thought I should have gotten used to the challenges along the way. My tears have often poured like rain, streaking through my soul to the thirsty earth, especially those times the thorns of life tore through my soul and my heart, till every fiber of my flesh writhes in pain. The good news is that in each of those difficult moments, God picked up my pieces, mended my heart, and cheered me on.

Every day I wake up, I press on, be it winter or summer, be it a time of famine or a season of prosperity; looking unto Jesus

"... the author and finisher of *our* faith, who for the joy that was set before Him endured the cross, despising the shame, and has sat down at the right hand of the throne of God" (Hebrews 12:2).

After coming thus far, my mind is made up. And no matter how fierce the battle gets, I will press on day after day till I cross the finish line, for I know in the end, it will be worth the fight. Why am I so confident that you and I, who have received Jesus as our Lord and Savior, will cross the finish line triumphantly? It's because Jesus defeated the devil about two thousand years ago, and with Him on our side, every devil on our way will suffer that defeat. All we have to do is "to trust and obey!"

It's a joy to know that we are not alone in this fight. The Captain of our salvation is fighting with us (Hebrew 2:10). Jesus knows our every weakness and problem. He is waiting to partner with you. He is waiting for you to surrender your life to Him, and by so doing, give Him the legal right to take over your battles. If you latch onto His outreached hands today, He will lift you up and lead you through the rest of your journey, one day at a time.

Quit fighting your battles alone. There is no greater friend like Jesus. He will not let you down. He will set you free and keep you free till the end of your life. John 8:36 says, **"Therefore if the Son makes you free, you shall be free indeed.**

CHAPTER NINE

THE SEVENTH LAW OF SELF-EXAMINATION

A prudent *man* foresees evil *and* hides himself;
The simple pass on *and* are punished.
- Proverbs 27:12

The seventh law of self-examination: ***What you defeat today will try other ways to reinvent itself in your life tomorrow.***

Many people start well in almost anything they set their hands to do. The problem is how far can they go? How much can they endure down the road when things get tough? The devil does not just leave you alone the first time you defeat him; he lays wait for your unguarded moments to attack again. How do you prepare for such times? How do you make sure you stay an overcomer?

REPEATING THE SAME MISTAKES

One victory over your enemy does not make you a hero. One good test score will not earn you a university or college degree.

Going to church once a year does not make you a churchgoer. In the same vein, making one mistake does not make you a failure. But when you repeat the same mistake over and over again, you will end up becoming a failure or defeated. So, without repeated victories over the devil and over sin, you will never be an overcomer.

Winning is a deliberate effort, a daily fight for your soul. It's not an accident, or something you fight for once in a while, hence the need for the daily life of self-examination. Job did not impress God with a one-time victory. It was his consistent life of victory that made God notice him and proudly boasts about him. "**Then the LORD said to Satan, "Have you considered My servant Job, that *there is* none like him on the earth, a blameless and upright man, one who fears God and shuns evil?" (Job 1:8).**

How prepared are you to cross the finish line? No casual trainer for an Olympic medal will ever be successful. To finish strong, you have to fight daily; you have to examine your steps and your life daily. Being watchful and prepared to fight the good fight of faith is one of the important keys to finishing strong (1Timothy 6:12).

It is sad to note that every day people fall out of fellowship with God. Some of them were very faithful to God for many years. Some of them were the shining lights in their offices, the beacons in their villages, and the stars that lighted their neighborhood until they succumbed to the repeated attacks of the devil. Some resisted taking bribes for years; some resisted fornication or adultery for years but did not realize that the devil does not give up. His method is to wear you out slowly or to overwhelm you suddenly.

My dear friend, be prepared every day because the devil is watching your every move. Always fix your eyes on the finish line, and see the present-day wiles or temptations as not comparable to the crown that awaits you in heaven. Always run the Christian race with the assurance that, if you don't faint and fall by the wayside, one day, the Lord will say to you, **"Well *done,* good and faithful servant; you were faithful over a few things, I will make you ruler over many things. Enter into the joy of your lord" (Matthew 25:21).**

PREVENTION

As the saying goes, "An ounce of prevention is better than a pound of cure," or "a stitch in time saves nine." The wise also say that "prevention is better than cure." It is important to always stop from time to time to ask yourself, "What are the things I can do today to prevent certain old habits or challenges from reinventing themselves in my life tomorrow?"

Self-examination is one of the greatest life-saving and preventive tools God gave us. It is the eye that sees what you will not ordinarily see; the sieve that stops dangerous tiny particles from getting into your food or system; the pill that bolsters your immune system and stops germs from overpowering or tearing down your body. So, no matter how many times and the various ways the devil tries to attack you, if you have strong barriers and preventive measures in place, or a light constantly illuminating your path or the loud warning bells of self-examination continually ringing in your ears, you will foil every of his plan.

Let's look at four areas of our lives we need to apply the stringent preventive measures daily; areas with very serious implications through which the devil attacks often and furiously. When problems are not prevented, they take roots downwards and bear fruits upwards; in other words, they develop strongholds.

Your health

Borrowing some lines from one of my books, ***The cardinal laws of freedom***, "One of the saddest things that can happen to a man is to go for his annual medical checkup and be told a few days later that he has terminal cancer, and that it has invaded his body over a while, and done damages unnoticed. Looking back, he probably would remember a few minor symptoms that cropped up in the past few months which he had dismissed as nothing."

It's easy to ignore minor symptoms. We assume they are nothing to worry about, but sometimes such assumptions can be dangerous and costly. As finite beings, there is a lot we don't know and we don't see. That's why, over the years, scientists have invented different tools and instruments to help us to see more of the invisible microbial and cellular world physically.

The hideous nature of some diseases underscores the fact that annual medical examination is essential to a healthy lifestyle and longevity. Unfortunately, many cannot afford a yearly medical checkup because they don't have medical insurance or the money to foot the medical bills. Sadly, many of them end up paying dearly for it, sometimes with their lives.

No matter how little, symptoms are necessary alarms that crop up to help warn us about the advent of insidious diseases. No matter how small, never ignore any symptoms. This is one major thing keeping the average lifespan of Africans lower than usual.

The good news is there is a checkup everyone can afford. This checkup does not require a physician's trained eyes and sophisticated instruments, nor does it place any financial burden on anyone. All that is needed is a few minutes of your time each day. This free and easy checkup is called ***Self-examination***. It's a good prophylactic measure both for physical and non-physical symptoms.

You are more likely to beat a storm if you are well equipped and prepared to fight it. Never, never let down your guards! Examine yourself regularly. That's the best way to keep healthy, physically and spiritually. Yes, with the little rudder of self-examination, you can steer the ship of your life through a quiet or stormy sea, but it's better to know what to do to avoid running into a storm in the first place. Storms are unpredictable. They have sunk many great ships and brought down many great planes, destroyed many strong houses, and ruined the lives of many great men and women.

Your heart

The heart is so important that the Bible instructs you, in Proverbs 4:23, to **"Keep your heart with all diligence, For out of it *spring* the issues of life."**

An unhealthy physical heart spells a lot of trouble. It threatens a person's entire life: his dreams, career, family, gifts, and purpose. The same is true for an unhealthy spiritual state of the heart. The heart is the most valuable thing God gave us. Without a good heart, you can never have a good life.

Usually, when you have valuable goods like gold and diamonds, you keep them in a safe place to protect them. You are not careless with them; you guard them with *all diligence.* The sad thing is that many of us would go to any length to secure our precious goods, but we let down our guards when it comes to our spiritual life. Unfortunately, by so doing, you are exposing yourself to a barrage of assaults and attacks from the devil. That explains why there are so many casualties in the spiritual race. Many lives are unguarded, and many lives are without the protective gears of God. The right armors are missing, making it easy for the devil to have a field day.

If you make a daily investment of self-examination in your life, you will keep your heart always guarded against the deadly arrows of the world and the devil that are aimed at destroying your Christian faith, your goods, and your life. Guarding your heart, therefore, is an issue of life and death. The discipline of self-examination will help you begin your day with prayer and the Word of God, and by so doing, you will give attention to the living Word of God, which can guard your heart and life.

"My son, give attention to my words;
Incline your ear to my sayings.
Do not let them depart from your eyes;
Keep them in the midst of your heart;
For they *are* life to those who find them,
And health to all their flesh."

Proverbs 4:20-22

Your habits

Many people will still be alive today if they had applied some basic preventive measures to certain areas of their lives. It is a well-documented fact that those who get good sleep, eat healthy diets, worry less, and exercise tend to live longer. That means that taking certain measures and engaging in certain good behaviors like examining the constitution of the food you eat to make sure it's good for your health will help prolong your life. In effect, life is all about cause and effect, actions and reactions, seedtime, and harvest time. If you sow the right prevention seeds today, you will reap the sweet harvest of good health and longevity tomorrow. And so is true for freedom. If you sow peace in your marriage, you will reap peace. If you sow love in your marriage, you will reap the harvest of love. But if you sow trouble and heartaches in your marriage, you will reap a whirlwind of troubles: pressed down, shaken together, and running over. Be careful what seeds you sow.

Prevention and self-examination are synonymous and

synergistic in many ways. They are two keys that open the same door. They are two life-changing paraphernalia you need in your everyday toolkit. They are light and salt in the lives of those that tap into their wells or treasure chest. They work together to illuminate a man's path and keep him preserved. Self-examination finds a crack; prevention repairs it and stops it from becoming a monster. Self-examination opens the door to a new and lovely path; prevention keeps the road from being littered with things that can make you stumble and fall. Self-examination finds a leak; prevention seals it quickly before it becomes a thoroughfare for disease and death. Self-examination points you to the right path of life, the path that will lead to peace and tranquility. It then hands the baton over to prevention to build a fence around you so that you can enjoy the peace and tranquility as you journey through life. You can never go wrong with being pointed to the right way, being alerted in time of an imminent danger, or being awakened from slumber through living a life of self-examination. Proverbs 12:28 says,

In the way of righteousness *is* life,
And in *its* pathway, *there is* no death.

Self-examination gives you a hearing ear, a hearing ear that is receptive to corrections and instructions from men and God. In effect, self-examination opens your ears to hear when God is speaking and where He is leading. **"Your ears shall hear a word behind you, saying, 'This *is* the way, walk in it,' Whenever you turn to the right hand or whenever you turn to the left" (Isaiah 30:21)**.

In the same vein, self-examination opens your eyes to see the way God wants you to go. Self-examination and prevention are in the life-saving business. Avail yourself of them, and you will have a pleasant and rewarding life. Always remember the scripture that says, **"A prudent *man* foresees evil *and* hides himself; The simple pass on *and* are punished" (Proverbs 27:12).**

Your morals

The Christian is a flag bearer, an embodiment of great virtues that redemption bestowed on us. The sad thing is that many of us do not realize what we carry. As a Christian, you represent everything Christ represents. You take His glory, His power, and His beauty everywhere you go. This is why the devil is after you. He wants to strip you of your power, testimony, Christlike character, and celebrity status. He wants to push you down from your exalted throne and rob you of your prized possessions. And one of the ways he tries to achieve this is by attacking your morality. The Christian has no message without good morals, no light, no value, no power, and influence. He becomes ordinary, lost in a world without morality.

Suppose you must keep your morals in check. In that case, you need the preventive pills of self-examination along with a consistent prayerful life, a constant life of fellowshipping with God through interacting with His Word, and corporate worship. The preventive pill of self-examination serves as a major deterrent to moral, social, emotional, and economic degradations. If you take them every day, they will prevent the crystallization of bad habits or the build-up of little plaques in the spiritual blood vessels of your Christian life. The weed you prevent from taking roots in your life today would save you the trouble of dealing with a forest in the future.

If you must prevent weeds from growing on the landscape of your heart, you must daily consecrate yourself. And in order to consecrate yourself, you have to first examine your heart and soul or take proper stock of your lifestyle and daily habits. Leviticus 11:44 says, **"For I *am* the LORD your God. You shall therefore consecrate yourselves, and you shall be holy; for I *am* holy. Neither shall you defile yourselves with any creeping thing that creeps on the earth."** The exercise of self-examination gives you the knowledge of the areas that need greater attention or mortification in your life.

Every day, pull open the drawers of your heart and look into it with the lens of self-examination for any cobwebs or roaches that are secretly gnawing the edges of your heart. What you prevent today will not fail to revisit your life tomorrow. If you truly want to present your body daily to God as a living sacrifice, you have to daily employ the tool of self-examination to help you prevent living a sin-infested life.

The Bible in Romans 12: 1-2 gives us a profound charge that calls for a daily re-examination of our lives. **"I beseech you therefore, brethren, by the mercies of God, that you present your bodies a living sacrifice, holy, acceptable to God, *which is* your reasonable service. And do not be conformed to this world, but be transformed by the**

renewing of your mind, that you may prove what *is* that good and acceptable and perfect will of God."

Self-examination is a duty, a call we must not ignore if we want to present ourselves as a holy, acceptable, and living sacrifice daily. It opens the door to freedom quicker than the bigger handles you may have tried to use to open your door of captivity. It's a small handle, but it can open almost every door of captivity for you to escape. It's a small key, but it can open every padlock that has shuttered the prison door that has held you captive for years. Those who constantly ignore self-examination will always pay great prices for doing so.

CHAPTER TEN

THE EIGHT LAW OF SELF-EXAMINATION

When I fixed My limit for it, And set bars and doors; When I said, 'This far you may come, but no farther...
- Job 38:10-11

The eighth law of self-examination: ***If you don't lock your doors, you will be besieged.***

It is hard for me to forget the day a rat crawling on my body woke me up from sleep. That was over forty years ago, but it's still fresh in my memory. It was during the Biafra-Nigeria civil war in the late sixties. At that time, sleep was a luxury as we were being ravaged by war. When I went to sleep that night, I was not expecting a rat to trouble my already troubled life. But I was jolted up that night by the intruder because there was an opening somewhere that was wide enough for the rat to crawl into our house.

At each giving time, there is always someone eager to invade your life or your body or your space, with the sole aim of disrupting your life and causing you pain. That's the job of the devil and his agents. Like the rat that crawled into my village house, they are always looking for ways to gain entrance into your life. This is why you must always lock your doors or plug every space through which the devil can gain entrance.

Stop the devil before he stops you!

Over the years, I have formed the habit of checking my doors before going to bed, and many times I have found one or two doors not locked. Who knows how much pain this simple habit has saved my family? Yes, most men do the same in their various homes. Well and good, but why do many professionals, intellectuals, respected businessmen and women, and other people who seem to have things together fail to examine their lives every day like they examine their bank accounts or the doors of their houses? Some people go as far as intentionally flinging the doors of their lives wide open, all day to the lust of the flesh, the lust of the eyes, the pride of life, and to all kinds of wandering demon spirits; forgetting that 1 Peter 5:8 says,

"Be sober, be vigilant; because your adversary the devil walks about like a roaring lion, seeking whom he may devour."

Some criminals specialize in staking out houses that might have unsecured doors to invade or burglarize. They sneak behind houses unnoticed, and in many cases, they find some back doors unsecured. Many have lost valuable items by keeping their back doors unlocked before going to bed or going to work. Some have even lost their lives through such carelessness. They left their doors unbolted; robbers came in and took their lives to make sure they were not identified or caught after stealing whatever they came to steal. In the same vein, many Christians have lost great intimacy or closeness with God for failing to secure the doors of their lives, be it their ears, their eyes, their mind, their heart, or their mouth. They made these important gateways to their soul and spirit a thoroughfare, an open highway where every vulture and wild beast can roam around and afflict them.

You are God's temple

It's important to know that we are the temple of God, a spiritual house, and we need to keep the doors of our temple locked up at the appropriate times to prevent the enemy of our life from invading us. The Bible asked an important question in 1 Corinthians 3:16-17,

"Do you not know that you are the temple of God and *that* the Spirit of God dwells in you? If anyone defiles the temple of God, God will destroy him. For the temple of God is holy, which *temple* you are."

It's as important to secure the temple of God as it is to secure your home. It is obvious from the above scripture that you have a very important assignment from God to ensure that your temple is not destroyed by you or by the enemies you advertently or inadvertently give access to your life.

There is even a very severe warning from God to those who destroy His temple. God is clearly and emphatically saying destroying His temple, which is your body, will attract His wrath. As clear as this warning is from God, yet many people trifle with their temple every day, permitting all kinds of people to lay hands on their heads or afflict them with demonic powers during purported prayers. Many people assimilate all sorts of ungodly visuals on the internet and TV. When you willfully open the doors of your life to gossip, jealousy, envy, hatred, and unforgiveness on a daily basis, you are submitting your temple to a gradual defilement and degradation.

As an emphasis, your house is the temple of God. Secure it every day through a life of self-examination. Examine the windows and doors of your life to make sure they are secured by the Holy Spirit every minute of the day. Don't leave your door wide open for the roaring lion to invade. There is a great assignment God has for you that the devil wants to abort. Don't let him have his way. Begin to secure your doors today through a daily life of self-examination and consecration, and you will fulfill your dreams and your God-given purpose in life.

If you lock your doors, you will keep your foes out. If you lock your doors, you will expunge woes from your life. If you lock your doors, your spiritual power will stop seeping out through the crevices that are left open. If you lock your doors, you will save yourself a lot of pain and heartaches by denying access to the enemy of your soul. If you lock your doors, you will keep your treasures safe, all the great treasures God has bestowed upon you.

The good news is that there is a key right now in your hand to lock your doors and that key is the knowledge of self-examination! Begin to use it every day to secure your doors, and your life will not remain the same; you will experience freedom as never before.

The greatest bolt

Many secure the doors of their lives with their college degrees or something that has no strength to stop the devil. In their mind, their college degrees have enough power to fend off any attack against them. To some, their job is their security; to some others, their wealthy friends or relatives in high places are their defense walls. This false sense of security makes them feel invincible, keeping the doors of their lives secured with things that cannot withstand the strong arm of the devil. What is your anchor? With what have you secured the doors of your life?

Some people have dabbled into mysticism and idolatry and have adapted them as a way of life. Some of them use charms, amulets, and other spiritual artifacts to protect themselves from the devil or their enemies. They use astral projections, demonic incantations, and invocations as weapons of defense. They put their trust in spiritual forces that are at war with God. Knowingly or unknowingly, they daily choose to bypass God to acquire demonic powers that have tremendous eternal consequences. Not only will the devil fail them when they need him most, but he will also keep them in captivity until their last day on earth unless they repent and give their lives to Jesus Christ, who was manifested to destroy the works of the devil (1 John 3:8).

The sad thing is that there are Christians who have not fully renounced satanic worship and cultures. In Africa, some village cultures make certain ungodly demands on their natives and, sometimes, settlers. And many African Christians, out of fear or lack of faith, still submit themselves to such idolatrous and satanic practices. For instance, in certain parts of Nigeria, after a woman gives birth, she has to bring her child to the village chief priest for some satanic rituals that are nothing but dedicating that child to her village's god. To date, many Christians from such villages are still submitting to this culture, bringing every of their child to the chief priest to dedicate to the village idol or god. To these supposed Christians, they have bought into the belief of the village that if they fail to do according to the customs of their village, they or their children will die. To them, they would rather trust their village idols than trusting the Almighty God. This prompts the question, "Who is the anchor of your life?" Read what the Bible says concerning dual loyalty. **"No servant can serve two masters; for either he will hate the one and love the other, or else he will be loyal to the one and despise the other. You cannot serve God and mammon" (Luke 16:13).**

The only safe anchor is Jesus Christ. And one of the strongest bolts He gave us to secure the doors of our life is prayer. Prayer is the bolt that will stop your enemies from invading your life and wreaking havoc. If you compliment the self-examination discipline with the virtue of prayer, you will never live a defeated life again.

Prayer gets God's attention more than anything else. The day you integrate self-examination with fervent prayer life, you will begin a relationship with God that you have never had before. The day you compliment your prayer life with a consistent lifestyle of self-examination, you will ignite a fire in your life that the world will notice; a fire that will consume every altar and horn raised against you; a fire that will reduce every door of opposition in your life to ashes.

The habit of self-examination has the power to give prayer a significant boost or momentum. Its combination with prayer can muster enough power to lift you above every mountain or obstacle. Their mixture can muster enough power to break every captive chain, and their collaboration can trigger a spiritual force strong enough to destroy twenty years of bad habits or slavery and set you completely free!

How God makes godly men and women

God makes great men and women through prayer. No intimate relationship can happen between a man and God without the man constantly tarrying in God's presence until the character of God is formed in him. That is why I pity men looking for other men to make them great. Every handiwork of man is imperfect; so, when a man makes you whatever you want him to make you, it's important to note that you are bound to inherit some of his flaws. But when God makes you, He takes His time to mold and shape you, and when He is done, you will not only be extraordinary, you will be a man who loves and carries His presence.

It's interesting to note that while so many people in authority are hardly accessible, the Almighty God, the creator of all visible and invisible things, gives everyone access to His presence. What is more? You can gain an audience with men in authority and leave empty-handed and disappointed. But you cannot come out of God's presence without being touched or changed. The more you stay in His presence in fervent prayer, the more His power transforms you. The more you tarry in His presence on your knees, the more He transforms you.

Great pair

Self-examination reminds you to pray, but prayer brings you to your knees, to a place of surrender, to the place where it's easy to hear when God speaks. Self-examination notifies you when your ears are clogged by pride, but prayer goes further. It keeps you in the presence of God until your ears are unclogged. Self-examination reminds you that your eyes are becoming clouded by the works of the flesh, but prayer goes further. It keeps you on your knees until the cloud is rolled away by the mighty hands of God.

Self-examination keeps you alert; prayer keeps you alive. Self-examination gives you structure; prayer gives you strength: the strength to prevail in your battles and set your enemies' armies to flight; the strength to be a light to your generation. Isaiah 40:31 says,

"But those who wait on the LORD
Shall renew *their* strength;
They shall mount up with wings like eagles,
They shall run and not be weary,

They shall walk and not faint."

Self-examination reveals your weaknesses; prayer uproots them from your life. Self-examination reminds you to build an altar of sacrifice, but prayer attracts the presence of God to your altar. Self-examination alerts you when you are getting spiritually weak, but the power of prevailing prayer rejuvenates your spirit and makes your hands strong again for battle.

The sharp eye of self-examination determines how safe a bridge is for you to cross, but prayer stops the bridge from caving in under you. The sharp eye of self-examination sees a door in your life that should not be left open, but prayer musters the force to close it and keep it closed. Self-examination reminds you to read your Bible, but prayer opens the eye of your understanding to comprehend the mysteries of the kingdom of God hidden from ordinary men and women.

Self-examination tells you when your life is filthy and smelly, but it takes prevailing prayer in the secret place where you always meet God to turn a smelly life into a life with a sweet aroma. So, treading the path of prayerlessness is treading on a dangerous path. It's like sailing without a rudder or paddle. It will be hard to make it through the unavoidable swift and turbulent currents of life along the way. Without a fervent prayer life, it will be hard to close the door through which the devil has always invaded your life.

It's a clear order, a command from God **"... that men always ought to pray and not lose heart" (Luke 18:1).** In this dangerous time and age, consistent life of self-examination and prayer will help you build a strong hedge around your life and your family. When you invest quality time to build a life of self-examination and prayer, you will attract the attention of men and the attention of heaven. When you invest quality time to build a life of self-examination and prayer, you will quickly discover that, when strong winds of life blow and uproot ordinary men, you will still be standing. When you invest quality time to build a life of self-examination and prayer, you will discover that battles of life are not necessarily won by beauty, talents, and gifts but are won on the knee, in the presence of God, where nothing can withstand the power of His glory and might.

Take that step

Embark on the wonderful and rewarding journey of self-examination and prayer today, knowing that **"The effective, fervent prayer of a righteous man avails much" (James 5:16).** Take that step: go daily to your prayer closet to hold the helm of God's garment until He closes every strange door in your life.

Hell is raging, enlarging, and engraving its handwriting everywhere. That's why Matthew 11:12 says, **"And from the days of John the Baptist until now the kingdom of heaven suffers violence, and the violent take it by force."**

A life of persistent prayer is not an option but an absolute necessity. It is the roadmap to being free and staying free. The life of self-examination is also not an option but a necessity. With these two virtues, you will live a daily life of victory and freedom. Take that step now. You can do it!

In one of my poems titled ***They said it can't be done***, I wrote:

So, they said it can't be done;
nobody will listen to you
because you have no money or fame,
and you bought it!

They said it can't be done
because you don't have the education
or the pedigree to make any difference,
and you bought it!

They said it can't be done
because you have no godfather
or someone in the corridors of power
to push you over the edge or to the top,
and you bought it!

Ah, mortal man, mortal man.
Who told you your faith and destiny
lie in the empty words of a man?

Did they not tell the fern,
"You are just a plant,
you can't grow on rocks?"
But it did.

Did they not tell the ivy,
"You are too slender,
you can't climb a wall or a tree?"

But it did.

Did they not tell the mustard seed,
"You are too small to grow
into a mighty tree?"
But it did.

Did they not tell the cactus,
"No plant that grows in the desert
lives longer than a few months?"
But it did.

Yes, they said it can't be done,
but that's the word of a mortal man.
If you believe it can be done,
one day, you too will prove them wrong.

Take that step today. Dare to walk on the path of self-examination. It will lead you to *freedom.* Dare to live a life of daily self-examination, and you will walk daily in freedom. You can do it!

PRAYER OF SALVATION

If you would like to accept Jesus as your personal Lord and Savior, pray this simple prayer by faith, and you will become a born-again child of God.

"Dear God, thank you for sending your Son to die on the cross for my sins. According to Your Word, if I acknowledge that You raised Jesus from the dead and that I accept Him as my Lord and Savior, I would be saved. Right now, I forsake my sins, and I accept Jesus as my personal Lord and Savior. Thank you for hearing my prayers, and forgiving my sins, and giving me a brand-new life. I confess and believe that from today, Jesus is my Lord and my Savior."

Congratulations! Welcome to the family of God's redeemed people. Join a church or a Christian fellowship to help you grow and mature in the Lord.

www.ingramcontent.com/pod-product-compliance
Lightning Source LLC
LaVergne TN
LVHW090958080826
845145LV00003B/1053

* 9 7 8 0 9 7 2 9 5 2 5 3 8 *